WORLD'S CLASSICS

═══

PLATO

Phaedo

═══

Translated and Edited by
DAVID GALLOP

Oxford   New York

OXFORD UNIVERSITY PRESS

1993

Oxford University Press, Walton Street, Oxford OX2 6DP

Oxford New York Toronto
Delhi Bombay Calcutta Madras Karachi
Kuala Lumpur Singapore Hong Kong Tokyo
Nairobi Dar es Salaam Cape Town
Melbourne Auckland Madrid

and associated companies in
Berlin Ibadan

Oxford is a trade mark of Oxford University Press

British Library Cataloguing in Publication Data
Data available

Library of Congress Cataloging in Publication Data
Plato.
[Phaedo. English]
Phaedo/Plato: translated and edited
by David Gallop.
p.   cm.—(World's classics)
Includes bibliographical references.
1. Immortality (Philosophy)—Early works to 1800.
I. Gallop, David. II. Title. III. Series.
B379.A5G34 1993 184—dc20 92–29711
ISBN 0–19–283090–2

1 3 5 7 9 10 8 6 4 2

Typeset by Cambrian Typesetters, Frimley, Surrey
Printed in Great Britain by
BPCC Paperbacks Ltd
Aylesbury, Bucks

PHAEDO

PLATO (c.427–347 BC), Athenian philosopher-dramatist, has had a profound and lasting influence upon Western intellectual tradition. Born into a wealthy and prominent family, he grew up during the conflict between Athens and the Peloponnesian states which engulfed the Greek world from 431 to 404 BC. Following its turbulent aftermath, he was deeply affected by the condemnation and execution of his revered master Socrates (469–399) on charges of irreligion and corrupting the young. In revulsion from political activity, Plato devoted his life to the pursuit of philosophy and to composing memoirs of Socratic inquiry cast in dialogue form. He was strongly influenced by the Pythagorean thinkers of southern Italy and Sicily, which he is said to have visited when he was about 40. Some time after returning to Athens, he founded the Academy, an early ancestor of the modern university, devoted to philosophical and mathematical inquiry, and to the education of future rulers or 'philosopher kings'. The Academy's most celebrated member was the young Aristotle (384–322), who studied there for the last twenty years of Plato's life.

Plato is the earliest Western philosopher from whose output complete works have been preserved. At least twenty-five of his dialogues are extant, ranging from fewer than twenty to more than three hundred pages in length. For their combination of dramatic realism, poetic beauty, intellectual vitality, and emotional power they are unique in Western literature.

DAVID GALLOP is Professor of Philosophy (Emeritus) at Trent University, Ontario. He taught philosophy at the University of Toronto (1955–69) and at Trent University (1969–89). He has also taught at Princeton University, at the University of Canterbury, New Zealand, and at the Australian National University, where he was visiting fellow at the Humanities Research Centre in 1985. Besides his edition of the *Phaedo* for the Clarendon Plato Series, his publications include *Parmenides of Elea* (Toronto, 1984) and *Aristotle on Sleep and Dreams* (Peterborough, Ontario, 1991).

CONTENTS

INTRODUCTION

PLATO'S life spanned the last quarter of the fifth century BC and the first half of the fourth. His childhood and early youth coincided with the disastrous conflict in which Athens and her allies were pitted against Sparta and other city-states of the Peloponnese, and which embroiled the Greek world from 431 to 404. The events of the war are graphically recorded by two contemporary historians, Thucydides and Xenophon. It ended in humiliation for Athens and the overthrow of her democratic government. A period of turmoil ensued, during which the city was terrorized by a brutal oligarchy, the infamous 'Thirty Tyrants'. The democracy was restored in 403, and initially acted with moderation. Four years later, however, it perpetrated an abominable crime in the judicial murder of Plato's much-loved friend and master, Socrates. That momentous event, if we are to believe an account of Plato's early career preserved in his (possibly spurious) Seventh Letter, was a turning-point in his life. Disillusioned with practical politics, and despairing of all existing systems of government, he devoted himself thenceforth to philosophy, which alone seemed to hold out any hope for the betterment of the human condition. After visiting Italy and Sicily when he was about 40 (c.387), he returned to Athens, where he founded the Academy for the pursuit of philosophical and scientific inquiry, and for the education of would-be 'philosopher kings', intellectually enlightened statesmen whose special nature and training were described at length in his *Republic*.

Plato's dialogues are a testament to his master's inspiration and unique personal example. Most feature Socrates as a principal character, though in some he plays a subordinate role, and in a work of Plato's old age, the *Laws*, he has disappeared altogether. The Platonic dialogues are by far the most lifelike portrayals of Socrates to have come down to us, although valuable memoirs of him by Xenophon, as well as an entertaining lampoon in Aristophanes' comedy, the *Clouds*, are also extant. Since the real Socrates wrote nothing and

Plato did not write in his own person, the question of how far the Platonic Socrates is faithful, in thought or character, to the historical figure, and how far a mouthpiece for Plato himself, remains a literary mystery of the first magnitude.

The events dramatized in the *Phaedo* took place in 399 BC, when Socrates was 70 and Plato probably in his late twenties. The dialogue contains a narrative of Socrates' last day on earth and of his execution, which followed his conviction by an Athenian court on charges of 'irreligion' and 'corrupting the young'. It forms a sequel to episodes from a pre-trial conversation and from Socrates' trial and imprisonment, presented in Plato's *Euthyphro*, *Apology*, and *Crito*, respectively. Those shorter works are usually and plausibly assigned to an earlier date than the *Phaedo*. While the chronology of Plato's dialogues remains controversial, it can safely be said that the *Phaedo* belongs to his artistic maturity. Though unlikely to be among his latest compositions, it shows him, both as a philosopher and as a dramatist, at the height of his powers.

For its combination of philosophical with literary genius the *Phaedo* has, indeed, no rival in Plato's entire output, with the sole exception of the *Symposium*, which is thought by many scholars to have been composed at about the same time. As studies of two fundamental human realities, love and death, the two dialogues complement each other in many ways. In both works qualities central to the discussion are personified by Socrates, and in both the dramatic action is directly relevant to the concept under investigation. Just as the *Symposium* explores the nature of love in the context of love relationships within the Socratic circle, so the *Phaedo* explores the nature of death, and the question of life after death, in the context of the master's execution. So memorable is Plato's narrative of that occasion that it is often taken to be no mere fictionalized version of a real event, but an authentic record of what took place; fiction has virtually acquired the status of fact.

By commemorating the death of Socrates, the *Phaedo* has earned a place in world literature that its author could never have foreseen. In antiquity Socrates' good-humoured serenity in the face of death was so greatly admired that it served, especially through its influence upon Stoic writers, to fix a certain conception of 'the true philosopher' permanently in the Western imagination. We owe to it, ultimately, our use of 'philosophical' to mean the endurance of necessary evils with patience and equanimity. In the Christian era the martyrdom of Socrates would be viewed as prefiguring the Crucifixion. Not for nothing was Plato destined to be reviled, in a later age, by Friedrich Nietzsche as 'a Christian before Christ' (*Twilight of the Idols*, 10.2). Indeed, had Socrates been the founder of a world religion instead of an intellectual discipline, our dialogue would rank among the most sacred of its scriptures.

Of all Platonic texts, the *Phaedo*, with its emphasis upon the care of the immortal soul and its invective against the body, provides perhaps the strongest basis for Nietzsche's perception. It has become almost a charter document for a certain world view, which may conveniently be dubbed 'dualistic'. For it is in this dialogue, especially, that a whole range of dualities, which have become deeply ingrained in Western philosophy, theology, and psychology over two millennia, received their classic formulation: soul and body, mind and matter, intellect and sense, reason and emotion, reality and appearance, unity and plurality, perfection and imperfection, immortal and mortal, permanence and change, eternal and temporal, divine and human, heaven and earth. These dualities and others were absorbed into Christianity, and have been transmitted across the centuries in its theological doctrines, spiritual values, and ethical teachings.

Although the example of Socrates remained by far the most important influence upon Plato, one other deserves to be mentioned. Cicero, writing in the last century BC, tells us that after Socrates' death, Plato travelled first to Egypt, and later to Italy and Sicily 'in order to become acquainted with the discoveries of Pythagoras' (*De Republica*, i. 16). Pythagoras was a sixth-century sage who had emigrated from Ionia to southern Italy more than a century before Plato's birth. He was the legendary founder of a religious and philosophical brotherhood, whose discoveries in mathematics, music, and astronomy were to make a powerful impression upon Plato.

According to Cicero, Plato spent much time with the Pythagoreans of southern Italy, and he acquired notebooks from Philolaus of Croton, who is mentioned in our text (61d–e), and who may have been responsible for the transmission of Pythagorean teaching to mainland Greece.

The *Phaedo* reflects Pythagorean influence in both its setting and its substance. Its prologue takes place in Phlius, a small town in the north-eastern Peloponnese, where there was a Pythagorean community. The main conversation is narrated by Phaedo of Elis to Echecrates, who was an adherent of Pythagorean philosophy. Simmias and Cebes, Socrates' chief interlocutors in the conversation, are visiting Athens from Thebes, where they have studied with Philolaus. Echoes of Pythagorean teachings or practices can be heard in Socrates' denunciation of bodily pleasures (64d–65a), his devotion to intellectual reasoning and spiritual purity (65b–66a, 67a–b, 69b–d), the prohibition of suicide (62b), the theory of reincarnation in animals (81e–82b), and the hypothesis of a spherical earth (97d–e, 108e–109a).

All these motifs bear out Cicero's testimony that Plato, out of singular affection for Socrates, 'interwove obscure and weighty Pythagorean learning on many subjects with Socrates' care and subtlety in argument' (*De Republica*, i. 16). They also suggest, like much else in the dialogue, that Plato could attribute positions to his fictional hero which the historical Socrates is unlikely to have held. In general, the *Phaedo* is better read as a philosophical memoir than as a biographical record. Even the famous passage in which Socrates rehearses the story of his intellectual development (96a–100a) is artfully contrived to serve a philosophical purpose, and may have little or no foundation in fact.

In its philosophical dimension, the dialogue combines two principal themes, both of which exemplify the dualism mentioned above. The first is the so-called 'theory of forms'. This expression is a modern collocation which does not correspond to any wording of Plato's own, but which usefully picks out a *leitmotif* recurring in many of his dialogues. As generally understood, the 'theory' postulates the existence of unique entities which are ideal exemplars of items familiar to us in this world: the Perfect Circle, the Just Society, the Ideal Bed, Absolute Beauty. These entities, designated 'forms', are supposedly 'laid up in heaven': they are perfect paradigms of which earthly circles, societies, beds, and beauties are imperfect copies. This interpretation is, to say the least, controversial, and only the barest sketch of a large and difficult subject can be attempted here. But because the forms are so prominent in the *Phaedo* and are basic to so much of its argument, something needs to be said about them.

They are introduced almost casually (65d–e, 74a), as already familiar to the speakers, and as affording a working hypothesis (100a, 101c, 107b) rather than as firmly established truth. Early in the discussion, when dwelling upon the tendency of the body to hamper the soul in its quest for truth, Socrates mentions objects grasped not with the senses but with the intellect alone. These include 'a just itself', 'a beautiful and a good', 'largeness, health, and strength' (65d–e). Later (74a) 'the equal itself' is contrasted with sensible equals, such as logs and stones, and it is argued that we must have possessed knowledge of 'the equal itself' before birth. The argument is soon extended to other forms (75c–d), including beauty, goodness, justice, and holiness, whose existence is strongly reaffirmed once again (76d–e). In the next phase of argument 'the beautiful itself' is said to be 'uniform alone by itself', remaining 'unvarying and constant, never admitting of change', by contrast with 'the many beautiful things, such as human beings or horses or cloaks' (78d–e). The existence of forms is also characterized as 'a hypothesis worthy of acceptance' (92d). Finally (100b), they are posited as 'reasons', to explain why sensible objects have the properties that they do, and they provide a framework for the argument which clinches the case for the soul's immortality (102b–107b).

What were these 'forms' and how did Plato conceive of them? Older commentators often called them 'ideas', a transliteration of one of the Greek words usually rendered 'form'. For a modern reader, however, 'idea' is liable to mislead. For the forms are in no way subjective or mind-dependent entities. Although they are apprehended *by* the mind, they do not exist merely *in* the mind. Rather, they are objectively real items, existing independently of any particular thinker or act of thought. In some of the passages just surveyed, as in other Platonic writings, they are depicted as immutable entities set against the world of ever-changing particulars, permanent realities of which sensible objects are mere fleeting appearances, objects of certain knowledge rather than of fallible opinion.

According to Aristotle (*Metaphysics*, 987b1–10, 1078b10–32), the theory of forms developed from inquiries by the historical Socrates into ethical concepts, such as 'good', 'just', or 'holy', quests of the sort depicted in several of Plato's earlier dialogues. Socrates had there asked such questions as 'what is holiness?', in order to obtain a paradigm or standard, whereby to determine whether particular actions, or specific kinds of action, were holy or not (*Euthyphro*, 6e). Traces of just such an origin for the theory can be seen in two passages of the *Phaedo* where forms are explicitly connected with 'the questions we ask and the answers we give' (75d, 78d). In answering such questions as 'what is beauty?', an independently existing object is postulated, of which the word 'beautiful' is the name. Somewhat as Socrates is the bearer of the name 'Socrates', or 'the man who Socrates is', so the form of beauty is the true bearer of the name 'beautiful', or (in terminology often used in the dialogues) 'the thing that beautiful is'.

The *Phaedo* was well known to Aristotle, and is usually taken to confirm his report that Plato went beyond Socrates in setting the forms 'apart' from sensible things. Although abstractions such as holiness or justice sometimes figure in earlier dialogues, in no previous work are they so sharply differentiated from their sensible instances. In the *Phaedo* they are treated as, in some sense, 'other' than items revealed to us through the senses. Objects such as equality, largeness, and health are spoken of as realities existing 'alone by themselves' (67a–b, 83a–b), transcending the familiar world of equal logs or stones, large animals, and healthy people. Each form is unique, a single 'one', contrasted with its many sensible instances, invisible to the bodily eye, but accessible to the intelligence, the mental organ which 'sees' it. Apprehension of forms is even occasionally described in the exalted language of religious communion or mystical experience (79d, 84a–b).

Why, and in what sense, were the Platonic forms 'separated'? The traditional answer, as already noted, is that sensible objects merely approximate to a perfection which they can never fully attain: logs or stones can be only roughly, never exactly, equal; pencilled lines can never be quite straight; chalk circles never perfectly round; human beings or societies never absolutely beautiful or just. The forms are 'separate' from our world because no item on earth can match their perfection: the perfect X, whatever X may be, is literally 'out of this world'.

Although that interpretation has virtually defined Platonism in Western tradition, there is curiously little in the *Phaedo* to support it. It is true that Socrates speaks (75a–b) of sensible equals 'striving' to attain the form, and being 'inferior' to it. But it is not clear that this means that they only approximate equality. The reason actually given (74b–c) for differentiating 'the equal itself' from equal logs or stones is not that the latter are only approximately equal, but that they do not provide an unambiguous standard of equality. Since logs or stones are evidently both equal and unequal, to different observers, or in relation to different items, or at different times, they no more exemplify equality than its opposite, and therefore cannot be identical with it. No sensible object can therefore provide the standard to which we implicitly refer when we judge that one log is equal to another. Yet such a standard must exist, unless all such judgements are subjective, lying merely 'in the eye of the beholder', or purely relative to the context or occasion of comparison (74b–c, 102b).

That the separated forms were intended to serve as standards is suggested also by Plato's terminology. They are designated not only by abstract nouns such as 'equality' or 'beauty', but by simple adjectives, often with the definite article and the pronoun 'itself': 'the equal', 'the beautiful itself'. Such phrases designate the form as a standard, to which implicit reference is made when sensible objects are judged to have the property in question. Somewhat as our judgement that a log is 'one metre long' makes implicit reference to *the* standard metre which ultimately determines 'what a metre is', so our judgement that one log is equal to another makes reference, whether we recognize this or not, to *the* equal, which provides the standard for 'what equals are'. Just as the name 'metre' belongs, primarily, to the standard metre, and other items are so called by virtue of their relationship to that standard, so 'the equal itself' is the true bearer of the name 'equal', and sensible equals are so called by virtue of their relationship to it. If there existed no objective standard of equality, it would be meaningless to call logs and stones 'equal', just as it would be meaningless to call them 'one metre long' if there existed no standard metre. Similar arguments will hold for the concepts of beauty, goodness, justice, holiness, and others (75c–d). These too we never find unambiguously exemplified by any person or action in ordinary experience. Yet, so the argument would run, there must exist an objective standard by which we judge people or their actions to be beautiful, just, or holy, if such predicates are to have any meaning for us at all.

The forms most prominent in the *Phaedo* belong to the domains of ethics and mathematics. They are the value concepts studied in moral philosophy, and the numerical or quantitative concepts basic to arithmetic and geometry. But in certain contexts the theory of forms appears to have a much wider scope. A form is sometimes posited as the single property, X-ness, shared by each of the many items called 'X', the one thing which has 'communion' with each of them (100d), or in which they all 'partake' (102b). Thus, in the *Republic* a form is posited for each set of items 'to which we apply the same name' (596a), and forms for 'bed' and 'table' are introduced. In this role, the form serves as what later came to be called a 'universal', a single abstract entity for every class of objects, which enables them to be described by the common nouns or adjectives of a general vocabulary.

The foregoing has suggested two distinct ways in which Platonic forms were conceived: (1) as standards or paradigms, and (2) as common properties or 'universals'. Critics have long debated the question whether these two conceptions were conflated, or even confused, by Plato himself. It has also been doubted whether he was seriously committed to the full range of forms that the second conception seems to require. Forms for artificial objects and for natural substances are mentioned seldom and only in special contexts. In the first part of the *Parmenides* qualms are voiced over the scope of the theory. The youthful Socrates of that dialogue confesses doubts as to whether there are 'separated' forms for man, fire, or water; and he fears lest he fall into 'a bottomless pit of nonsense', if they are admitted for hair, mud, or dirt (130b–d). In the same dialogue separated forms, including some of those prominent in the *Phaedo*, are subjected to severe logical criticism. It has therefore been questioned whether the doctrine of separated forms retained Plato's allegiance. Many scholars believe that the theory underwent a radical revision in his later thought.

When he wrote the *Phaedo*, however, the separated forms were fundamental to his enterprise, providing the true subject-matter of philosophical inquiry. In Plato's Academy the Socratic quest for definitions was to be transformed into a programme of research, in which philosophical problems would be explored and settled with the objectivity and deductive rigour of mathematics. This programme and the methods proper to it are variously described in the dialogues of Plato's middle and later career. We glimpse the procedure envisaged at the time of the *Phaedo* in the new method of 'hypothesis', which Socrates briefly describes and applies to the forms themselves (100a–b, 101c–e). By articulating a disciplined understanding of those realities, Plato intended that the blind, fallible intuitions of ordinary human opinion should be replaced by firmly grounded scientific knowledge.

The second major dualistic theme in the *Phaedo* is the opposition between body and soul. Here too the dialogue has had an enduring influence. Its teaching largely anticipates the Christian conception of the soul as a spiritual substance, conjoined with the body during life, separated from it at death, and capable of existing thereafter in a disembodied state for all eternity. Sometimes soul–body dualism in the

Phaedo is seen also as an ancient forerunner of the view, stemming in modern philosophy from Descartes, that the mind is a simple, immaterial substance, a pure subject of thought and perceptual consciousness, which possesses no properties in common with physical objects extended in space. Yet to identify the 'soul' of the *Phaedo* either with the 'soul' of religious teaching or with the 'mind' of modern philosophical dualism is to oversimplify. The Greek concept of 'soul' (*psuchē*) is by no means straightforward, nor is it exactly commensurate with our own. Because our dialogue contains an amalgam of several different ideas, it will be worth glancing briefly at the most important of these.

In some places the soul is the 'true self', or 'real person'. As such, it is sharply distinguished from the individual's body (especially at 115c–e). It is that precious element in us whose good condition constitutes our true well-being. Its nurture is of paramount importance for our lives and should override all other human concerns. This line of thought, which is authentically Socratic, is given new emphasis in the *Phaedo* by stressing the ways in which the body is a constant hindrance to the well-being of the soul, and by insisting that nurture of the soul is important not only for earthly life but for the life to come. These doctrines impart a peculiar 'other-worldly' tone to much of the dialogue, and (as noted earlier) a hostility towards the body that is more pronounced in the *Phaedo* than in any other Platonic work.

The 'true self' conception of the soul, however, plays virtually no part in the arguments for its immortality. These draw, rather, upon two further ideas. The first is that of the soul as human reason or intellect, seeking wisdom or knowledge, and apprehending truth in acts of mental 'vision' (65b–c, 67c). In this capacity it is credited with prenatal knowledge of the forms (76c–e) and with other modes of rational activity (94b–d). The operations of 'soul' in this sense are limited to the intellectual and reasoning functions of human beings. In certain contexts, however, it seems conceived far more broadly as a 'life-principle' or source of vital energy, which 'brings life' to whatever body it occupies (105c–d). In this role the soul is not restricted to human beings, but animates organic things in general (70d), accounting for the differences between them and non-living objects. This second idea underlies the definition of death as 'separation of soul from body' (64c), and appears in both the first and the last of the arguments for immortality (69e–72e, 102a–107b).

These different pictures of the soul leave unclear just what is at issue in the discussion of immortality. What is it whose immortality is being established? What aspects of organic or mental life are supposed to survive bodily death? If pressed, these questions will be found to generate severe difficulties. For example, as an agent of change in living bodies, the soul is itself subject to change (79c, 81b–c, 83d–e). Yet as a pure intellect it is akin to the unchanging forms which it knows (80b). Again, the notion of reincarnation in animals (82a–b) sits uncomfortably with the idea of the soul as pure reason or intellect. The latter idea is also hard to square with Socrates' faith in personal survival, especially if that is taken to include emotions or memories of earthly experience, as described in the myth of the afterlife (114a–b). The dialogue contains, moreover, several widely disparate images of the soul: it is a 'prisoner' within the body (62b, 67d, 82e–83a); it can 'rule and be master' of the body (80a, 94b–e); it can even be 'weighed down' and appear in graveyards as a ghost (81c–d), or be fastened to the body 'with a sort of rivet' and made corporeal (83d). Yet no attempt is made to reconcile these images in a single coherent doctrine.

One fundamental difficulty, however, is directly confronted. Is it correct to assume that we are, as Socrates put it, 'part body and part soul' (79b)? Is the soul rightly conceived as an independent substance, capable of existing apart from the body? For a modern reader, even to ask whether the 'soul' is immortal may seem to pose the question of survival after death in antiquated and question-begging terms. Since the very word 'soul' refers to an entity which survives death, it may be thought that the question of the soul's immortality is pre-empted by that of its existence. Are the vital and mental functions of human beings rightly attributed to an incorporeal, separable substance called 'the soul'? Can it be doubted that those functions are exercised only under certain highly specific bodily conditions? Is it credible, or even intelligible, that mental life should continue once those conditions cease to obtain?

Such questions are raised, in effect, by Simmias' hypothesis that the soul is merely an 'attunement' of the bodily parts, comparable with the tuned state of a musical instrument (85e–86d). Just as it would be absurd to suppose that the tuned state of a lyre could exist when the instrument had been severely damaged or destroyed, so it is absurd to suppose that the soul could exist apart from the body. This remarkable theory effectively challenges the dualistic assumption underlying Socrates' arguments. In confronting him with it, and in giving him three refutations of it (92a–95a), Plato treats it as a serious and attractive rival to the dualistic view. It has, indeed, much plausibility, as Simmias says (92d); and it was to have many later descendants in philosophical accounts of the mind which have denied its separate existence either as causally impossible or as logically absurd.

The conception of the soul dominant in the *Phaedo* differs from Christian belief about it in one notable respect. Socrates is made to argue not only that it will continue to exist after death, but also that it already existed before birth. This conclusion is derived (73a–76e) from the theory of 'recollection' (*anamnēsis*), an intriguing doctrine which has had a perennial fascination for students of Plato. The theory that what we call 'learning' is really the regaining of knowledge which the soul possessed in a prenatal, disembodied state is often regarded as quintessentially Platonic. It has inspired poets as well as philosophers, and has resonances in much later theorizing about teaching and learning. Many who would not subscribe to a theory of prenatal existence have nevertheless believed the doctrine of recollection to contain deep insight into the cognitive powers of the mind.

Yet despite its appeal, the doctrine remains mysterious. When Socrates argues that in using our senses we 'regain' knowledge of what we had known before birth (75e, 76e), what exactly has he in mind? He is sometimes taken to mean that, in order to be able to recognize objects as having properties such as equality, we must have had a prenatal acquaintance with the forms of those properties. We draw upon that acquaintance whenever we exercise our normal ability to recognize sensible things as equal and to describe them as such. On such a view, 'recollection' is at work in the acquisition of concepts by anyone who learns a language, and it is exemplified in any ordinary act of recognition. Whenever we recognize or describe some sensible object as having a certain property, we are comparing it, albeit unconsciously, with a prenatally known form of that property. Just as we could not recognize or assess a portrait of Simmias as a likeness of him unless we had seen Simmias himself, so we could not recognize equal logs or stones as such, or assess their equality, unless we had had a prior (and prenatal) acquaintance with 'the equal itself'.

But that interpretation may not do justice to the doctrine, or at least may fail to capture its full intent. As already noted, the argument is extended only to a certain range of forms for mathematical and value concepts (75c–d). Moreover, stress is placed upon the ability to 'give an account' of those forms, which Socrates may be the only person to possess (76b). This presumably refers to his unique capacity for giving an account of ethical and quantitative concepts, or eliciting understanding of them by skilful questioning of others. 'Recollection' of that sort seems to involve not so much the acquisition and use of concepts by normal speakers of a language, as the philosophical work of clarifying concepts that have already been acquired. That way of understanding 'recollection' would bring our text closer to a well-known episode in the *Meno*, to which the *Phaedo* may contain an allusion (73a–b). In the *Meno* (81e–86b) Socrates elicits from a slave, previously unversed in geometry, the right solution to a geometrical problem. There too the process of recovering knowledge latent within the mind is explained as the retrieval from memory of truths known before birth, and it is used as a model for philosophical inquiry. Although the two passages differ in important ways, both point towards a mode of learning, found especially in mathematics and philosophy, which depends upon the mind's inherent reasoning powers rather than upon sense experience. Sensible objects serve merely as stimuli enabling learners to recover knowledge that is, in some sense, already present within them.

In a partly analogous way, Plato's writings afford a stimulus to the intellect, 'reminding' their readers of truths already familiar to them. Just as sensible objects may remind an observer of things previously known, so the dialogues contain verbal images by which the forms may be recollected, through their embodiment in the characters and dramatic action. Socrates compares his own quest for truth with the procedure of those who study an eclipse of the sun through images in water (99d). Theoretical discourse provides images of abstract truths superior to those provided by sensible objects (100a). Likewise, Plato's dialogues provide images of philosophical truths on a higher plane than items of sensory observation, and thereby make possible the 'recollection' of those truths by an attentive and reflective reader.

One recent writer has gone so far as to characterize the great dialogues of Plato's maturity as 'theatre; but theatre purged and purified of theatre's characteristic appeal to powerful emotion, a pure crystalline theatre of the intellect'.[1] Yet with respect to the *Phaedo*, at least, it is hard to agree entirely with this judgement. Plato did, to be sure, condemn the emotional excesses of the Athenian theatre, and he composed his dialogues partly as a cultural counterweight to conventional drama. Unlike classical Greek tragedy and comedy, they are written entirely in prose, often in the idiom of everyday conversation, and they lack the formal structures of tragedy and comedy. They self-consciously transcend both those genres, and their appeal is indeed largely intellectual. But the intellect is frequently engaged through episodes of intense emotional power, in which theoretical issues are brought to life and felt by the reader as matters of urgent personal concern.

The *Phaedo* provides one of the finest examples. In its dramatic action and in its preoccupation with human mortality, it comes closest of all Plato's writings to tragedy. It depicts a monstrous injustice committed, in the name of justice, against

---

[1] M. C. Nussbaum, *The Fragility of Goodness* (Cambridge, 1986), 133.

one who least of all deserved to suffer it; and it registers the anguish felt in face of that iniquity by those who loved him. By the end of the dialogue every person in the drama has evinced grief for Socrates: his emotional disciple Apollodorus (59b), his wife Xanthippe (60a), his jailer (116d), his friends Phaedo and Crito (117c–d), and finally the whole company except for Socrates himself. Their responses have always stirred compassion in readers of sensibility, and were surely meant to do so.

Such feelings are enhanced by Plato's artistry. It is no accident that Socrates takes a dream bidding him 'make art and practise it' to refer to 'art in the popular sense' (60e–61a). This, together with his thought that a true poet should 'make tales rather than true stories' (61b), reflects Plato's own poetic practice. The dialogue abounds in 'tales', ranging from Socrates' light-hearted story about pleasure and pain (60c) to the solemn myth of the afterlife with which he concludes (107c–115a). In a tale of poignant beauty, he compares himself with the prophetic swans of Apollo, who sing for joy at the prospect of their death (85a–b). Most moving of all, even for those who have read it many times, is the tale of his death (115b–118a). Its impact is due, in part, to its sheer restraint. Plato's control over language mirrors his master's self-control, the conquest of emotion by reason which the true philosopher embodies. But feelings of grief and fear, if they are to be mastered, need to be felt and acknowledged as the powerful forces that they are. Cebes had suggested that there lurks 'a child inside us' who fears death as if it were a bogeyman, and that the fear needs to be 'charmed' out of him by the singing of spells (77e). The *Phaedo* as a whole is Plato's incantation to his readers (114d), and the death scene forms its climax, the moment at which exorcism of the 'bogey' is finally achieved. Facing a universal human terror, Socrates triumphs over it with miraculous nobility of spirit. He displays the 'true bravery' and 'true temperance' which were aligned with wisdom earlier in the discussion (68b–69a). Wisdom is achieved through spiritual liberation, in which the emotions have been purified or purged away (69c, 82d). Yet only a reader who has shared, in some degree, the grief of

Socrates' companions will recognize the measure of that achievement.

In 1883 an editor of the *Phaedo* could remark that 'few products of Greek philosophy have been read more widely and less intelligently'.[2] The first part of that judgement, at least, remains unquestionable. Over the past century, however, admiration for the dialogue has been qualified. Its earnest defence of the philosophic life, austere moralizing, and edifying tone are not to the taste of every modern reader. To some the work has even seemed curiously 'unSocratic'. For whereas Socrates in the *Apology* (40c–41c, 42a) had remained non-committal concerning immortality, in the *Phaedo* he devoutly proclaims his faith in it. The speculations of the closing myth seem strangely out of character for the agnostic gadfly of the *Apology*. Even the dialogue's arguments are unlikely to strengthen the faith of those who believe in personal immortality, let alone convert those who do not. Those arguments rely, as we have seen, upon Academic tenets which go well beyond anything likely to have been maintained by the historical Socrates. In all these ways the *Phaedo* can be contrasted with Plato's more tentative earlier writings. It tends, not unnaturally, to be discussed as if it were a treatise, in which 'original doctrines' or 'positive teachings' of Plato's own are set forth for the first time.

Yet the *Phaedo* is not a treatise, and the contrast with earlier dialogues should not be overdrawn. In particular, the Socratic commitment to the give-and-take of rational discussion is still in evidence. The inquiry is conducted in a tolerant, unassertive manner, generously welcoming of doubt and disagreement. Socrates remains rationality incarnate, insisting that his argument leaves room for 'many misgivings and objections' (84c–d), urging his friends not to pull their punches (91c), and carefully restating their objections, so that they may be fairly treated (91c–d, 95b–e). At the end of the conversation he emphasizes the provisional character of the conclusion by encouraging his interlocutors to re-examine their basic premisses (107a–b). The true Socratic spirit can be

---

[2] R. D. Archer-Hind, *The* Phaedo *of Plato* (London, 1883), 44.

heard, above all, in his warning against 'misology' or distrust of argument, and in a suggestive comparison between the appraisal of arguments and the judgement of human character (89c–91c).

It is in that spirit that the dialogue still asks to be read. The probing of arguments, and of the philosophical problems which lie beneath their surface, is a task for all who would engage with Plato's dialogues on their own ground. In that respect the *Phaedo* is no different from the rest of the Platonic corpus. To study a Platonic text is to participate in a rewarding philosophical adventure. That observation holds as true for this dialogue as for others; and it remains as true today as when the *Phaedo* was written.

NOTE ON THE TEXT

THE original version of this translation was published in the Clarendon Plato Series in 1975 and was designed to be used in conjunction with a lengthy commentary. For the World's Classics edition it has been altered in a number of passages which would be unintelligible without the commentary. I have also taken the opportunity to make some improvements, often in the light of suggestions from reviewers of the original. The present version is occasionally somewhat freer than the earlier one, and will, I hope, be more accessible for readers coming to the *Phaedo* for the first time.

The explanatory notes are designed to make the translation intelligible and to enable the argument to be followed. They do not signal all of the many places in which Plato's text or its exact meaning remains uncertain. In a number of places, however, especially where the uncertainty significantly affects interpretation of the argument, alternative translations have been given in the notes, together with a brief indication of the point at issue.

The numbers and letters in the margin of the translation derive from a sixteenth-century edition of Plato's works by Henricus Stephanus. They are used universally by modern commentators for references to Plato's text, and are so used in the introduction and notes to this volume.

The translation is based on J. Burnet's Oxford Classical Text (1900), but deviates from it in the following nineteen places: 65e7, 66b3–4, 69a6–c3, 70d2, 71b2, 73c5–6, 74c13, 75d2, 82d3, 83b8–9, 83e6, 92d9, 96e9, 104d3, 105b9, 108a5, 112c3, 113c1, 115a2–3. The textual difficulties in these passages have seemed too minor or too technical for discussion in the present edition, but interested readers may consult the relevant notes in the Clarendon Plato volume.

A revised Oxford Classical Text of all Plato's works is in preparation. Its first volume, which includes the *Phaedo*, will appear in 1993, but the present translation has not been adjusted at points where the new text may diverge from Burnet's.

I am most grateful to my colleagues Fred and Annette Tromly, and to Michael Woods, general editor of the Clarendon Plato Series, for commenting upon the revised translation and upon new material written for this edition.

BIBLIOGRAPHICAL NOTE

THE literature on Plato is voluminous, and the *Phaedo* has attracted more commentary than almost any other dialogue. The bibliography lists only a small selection of modern works in English. These have been chosen partly to guide readers who are relatively unfamiliar with Plato, and partly for those who wish for more detailed commentary on the *Phaedo* than the present edition provides.

It is often worth consulting alternative translations, especially in difficult or controversial passages. Item 1 conveniently contains all Plato's works in a single volume. Several modern versions of the *Phaedo* have been listed in items 2–8. They contain English only, except for item 3 which includes a facing-page Greek text. Items 2, 4, and 6 contain substantial commentaries. The versions in 5, 7, and 8 are prefaced by useful short introductions.

Items 9 and 10 are, respectively, the Oxford Classical Text (1900) on which the present translation is based, and the first volume of a revised Oxford Classical Text (1993).

Items 11–13 contain an annotated Greek text but no translation. Items 14 and 15 are full-length philosophical studies of the *Phaedo*, written from very different perspectives and requiring no knowledge of Greek.

Item 16 deals with the circumstances surrounding Socrates' trial and condemnation, and 17 with the problem of disentangling his thought from that of Plato.

Items 18 and 19 contain simple outlines of Plato's life and thought; the former includes the famous Seventh Letter upon which all modern reconstructions of his life depend. Item 20 is a short critical assessment of him as a philosopher, and 21 is a lucid conspectus of his work by a leading twentieth-century British philosopher.

Items 22–9 are works of wider scope than the *Phaedo* but contain chapters especially relevant to it. These require no knowledge of Greek, although some are written at a fairly advanced level. The studies of specific problems or passages in 30–6 are also advanced, and some of them require knowledge of Greek.

Valuable literary and historical background for the appreciation of Plato will be found in items 37 and 38.

SELECT BIBLIOGRAPHY

COMPLETE WORKS OF PLATO

1. E. Hamilton and H. Cairns, eds. *The Collected Dialogues of Plato* (New York, 1961)

TRANSLATIONS OF THE *PHAEDO*

2. R. S. Bluck, *Plato's* Phaedo, translation with commentary (London, 1955)
3. H. N. Fowler, Loeb Classical Library, Plato, vol. i (London and New York, 1914)
4. D. Gallop, *Plato* Phaedo, translation with commentary (Oxford, 1975)
5. G. M. A. Grube, *Plato's* Phaedo (Indianapolis, 1977)
6. R. Hackforth, *Plato's* Phaedo, translation with commentary (Cambridge, 1955)
7. H. Tredennick, *The Last Days of Socrates* (Harmondsworth, 1954)
8. W. D. Woodhead, *Plato, Socratic Dialogues* (London, 1953)

GREEK TEXTS

9. J. Burnet, ed. *Platonis Opera*, vol. i (Oxford, 1900)
10. W. S. M. Nicoll *et al.*, eds. ibid. (Oxford, 1993)

EDITIONS OF THE *PHAEDO*

11. R. D. Archer-Hind. *The* Phaedo *of Plato* (London, 1883; 2nd edn. 1894; New York, 1973)
12. J. Burnet, *Plato's* Phaedo (Oxford, 1911)
13. W. D. Geddes, *The* Phaedo *of Plato* (London, 1863)

COMMENTARIES ON THE *PHAEDO*

14. D. Bostock, *Plato's* Phaedo (Oxford, 1986)
15. K. Dorter, *Plato's* Phaedo (Toronto, 1982)

BOOKS ON SOCRATES

16. C. D. C. Reeve, *Socrates in the* Apology (Indianapolis, 1989)
17. G. Vlastos, *Socrates, Ironist and Moral Philosopher* (Cambridge, 1991)

SELECT BIBLIOGRAPHY

INTRODUCTIONS TO PLATO

18. R. S. Bluck, *Plato's Life and Thought, with a translation of the Seventh Letter* (London, 1949)
19. G. C. Field, *The Philosophy of Plato*, 2nd edn. (Oxford, 1969)
20. R. M. Hare, *Plato*, Past Masters Series (Oxford, 1982)
21. G. Ryle, s.v. 'Plato', *Encyclopaedia of Philosophy*, ed. P. Edwards (New York, 1967), vi. 320–4

OTHER BOOKS

22. I. M. Crombie, *An Examination of Plato's Doctrines* (London, 1963), i. 303–24
23. J. C. B. Gosling, *Plato* (London, 1973), ch. 10
24. W. K. C. Guthrie, *A History of Greek Philosophy* (Cambridge, 1975), vol. iv, ch. 6
25. R. Robinson, *Plato's Earlier Dialectic* (Oxford, 1953), chs. 7, 9
26. T. M. Robinson, *Plato's Psychology* (Toronto, 1970), ch. 2
27. W. D. Ross, *Plato's Theory of Ideas* (Oxford, 1951), ch. 3
28. A. E. Taylor, *Plato, the Man and his Work* (London, 1929), ch. 8
29. N. White, *Plato on Knowledge and Reality* (Indianapolis, 1976), ch. 3

ARTICLES

30. J. L. Ackrill, '*Anamnesis* in the *Phaedo*: Remarks on 73c–75c', *Exegesis and Argument*, eds. E. N. Lee, A. P. D. Mourelatos, and R. Rorty (Assen, 1974), 177–95
31. J. Gosling, 'Similarity in *Phaedo* 73 seq.', *Phronesis*, 10 (1965), 151–61
32. D. O'Brien, 'The Last Argument of Plato's *Phaedo*', *Classical Quarterly*, 2nd series, 17 (1967), 198–231, 18 (1968), 95–106
33. K. M. W. Shipton, 'A Good Second-Best. *Phaedo* 99b ff.', *Phronesis*, 24 (1979), 33–53
34. C. Stough, 'Forms and Explanation in the *Phaedo*', *Phronesis*, 21 (1976), 1–30
35. G. Vlastos, 'Reasons and Causes in the *Phaedo*', *Philosophical Review*, 78 (1969), 291–325, repr. in *Platonic Studies* (Princeton, 1981), 76–110
36. —— '*Anamnesis* in the *Meno*', *Dialogue*, 4 (1965), 143–67

LITERARY AND HISTORICAL BACKGROUND

37. E. R. Dodds, *The Greeks and the Irrational* (Berkeley, 1951), esp. chs. 6–7
38. G. C. Field, *Plato and his Contemporaries* (London, 1930)

SYNOPSIS OF THE *PHAEDO*

PHAEDO

Echecrates. Were you there with Socrates yourself, 57
Phaedo,* on the day he drank the poison* in the prison, or
did you hear of it from someone else?

Phaedo. I was there myself, Echecrates.*

Echecrates. Then what was it that he said before his 5
death? And how did he meet his end? I'd like to hear about
it. You see, hardly anyone from Phlius goes to stay at
Athens nowadays, and no visitor has come from there for a b
long time who could give us any definite report of those
events, beyond the fact that he died by drinking poison;
there was nothing more they could tell us.

Phaedo. Didn't you even learn, then, about how the 58
trial went?

Echecrates. Yes, someone did report that to us, and we
were surprised that it was evidently long after it was over
that he died. Why was that, Phaedo? 5

Phaedo. It was chance in his case, Echecrates: it just
chanced that on the day before the trial the stern of the ship
that Athenians send to Delos had been wreathed.

Echecrates. What ship is that?

Phaedo. According to Athenian legend, it's the ship in 10
which Theseus once sailed to Crete, taking the famous
'seven pairs', when he saved their lives and his own as well. b
It is said that at that time the Athenians had made a vow to
Apollo that if they were saved, they would, in return,
dispatch a mission to Delos* every year; and this they have
sent annually ever since, down to this day, in honour of the 5
god. Once they've started the mission, it is their law that
the city shall be pure during that period, which means that
the state shall put no one to death, till the ship has reached
Delos and returned; and that sometimes takes a long time, c
when winds happen to hold them back. The mission starts
as soon as the priest of Apollo has wreathed the stern of the
ship; and, as I say, that chanced to have taken place on

1

the day before the trial. That's why Socrates spent a long
5 time in prison between his trial and death.

Echecrates. And what about the circumstances of the
death itself, Phaedo? What was it that was said and done,
and which of his intimates were there with him? Or would
the authorities allow no one to be present, so that he met
his end isolated from his friends?

d   *Phaedo.* By no means: some were present, in fact quite
a number.

Echecrates. Please do try, then, to give us as definite a
report as you can of the whole thing, unless you happen to
be otherwise engaged.

Phaedo. No, I am free, and I'll try to describe it for
5 you; indeed it's always the greatest of pleasures for me to
recall Socrates, whether speaking myself or listening to
someone else.

Echecrates. Well, Phaedo, you certainly have an audi-
ence of the same mind; so try to recount everything as
minutely as you can.

e   *Phaedo.* Very well then. I myself was curiously affected
while I was there: it wasn't pity that visited me, as might
have been expected for someone present at the death of an
intimate friend; because the man seemed to me happy,
Echecrates, both in his manner and his words, so fearlessly
5 and nobly was he meeting his end; and so I felt assured that
even while on his way to Hades he would not go without
divine providence, and that when he arrived there he would
59 fare well, if ever anyone did. That's why I wasn't visited at
all by the pity that would seem natural for someone present
at a scene of sorrow, nor again by the pleasure from our
being occupied, as usual, with philosophy—because the
5 discussion was, in fact, of that sort—but a simply extra-
ordinary feeling was upon me, a sort of strange mixture of
pleasure and pain combined, as I reflected that Socrates
was shortly going to die. All of us there were affected in
much the same way, now laughing, now in tears, one of us
b quite exceptionally so, Apollodorus—I think you know the
man and his manner.*

Echecrates. Of course.

Phaedo. Well, he was completely overcome by that state; and I myself was much upset, as were the others.

Echecrates. And just who were there, Phaedo?   5

Phaedo. Of the local people there was this Apollodorus, and Critobulus and his father,* and then there were Hermogenes, Epigenes, Aeschines, and Antisthenes;* Ctesippus of the Paeanian deme* was there too, and Menexenus* and some other local people. Plato, I believe,   10 was unwell.*

Echecrates. Were there any visitors there?

Phaedo. Yes: Simmias of Thebes, and Cebes and   c Phaedondes;* and Euclides and Terpsion from Megara.*

Echecrates. What about Aristippus and Cleombrotus?* Were they there?

Phaedo. No, they weren't; they were said to be in Aegina.*

Echecrates. Was anyone else there?   5

Phaedo. I think those were about all.

Echecrates. Well then, what discussion do you say took place?

Phaedo. I'll try to describe everything for you from the beginning. Regularly, you see, and especially on the   d preceding days, I myself and Socrates' other companions had been in the habit of visiting him; we would meet at daybreak at the court-house, where the trial was held, as it was close to the prison. We used to wait each day till the   5 prison opened, talking with one another, as it didn't open very early. When it did, we would go in to Socrates and generally spend the day with him. On that particular day we'd met earlier still; because when we left the prison the   e evening before, we learnt that the ship had arrived from Delos. So we passed the word to one another to come to our usual place as early as possible. When we arrived, the door-keeper who usually admitted us came out and told us   5 to wait, and not to go in till he gave the word; 'because', he said, 'the Eleven* are releasing Socrates, and giving orders that he's to die today.' But after a short interval he came back and told us to go in. On entering we found Socrates,   60

3

just released, and Xanthippe—you know her—holding his little boy* and sitting beside him. When she saw us, Xanthippe broke out and said just the kinds of thing that
5 women are given to saying: 'So this is the very last time, Socrates, that your good friends will speak to you and you to them.' At which Socrates looked at Crito and said: 'Crito, someone had better take her home.'

So she was taken away by some of Crito's people, calling
b out and lamenting; Socrates, meanwhile, sat up on the bed, bent his leg, and rubbed it down with his hand. As he rubbed it, he said: 'What an odd thing it seems, friends, this
5 state that people call "pleasant"; and how curiously it's related to its supposed opposite, "painful": to think that the pair of them refuse to visit a person together,* yet if anybody pursues one of them and catches it, he's always pretty well bound to catch the other as well, as if the two of
c them were attached to a single head. I do believe that if Aesop had thought of them, he'd have made up a story telling how God wanted to reconcile them* in their quarrelling, but when he couldn't he fastened their heads together, and that's why anybody visited by one of them is
5 later attended by the other as well. That is just what seems to be happening in my own case: there was discomfort in my leg because of the fetter, and now the pleasant seems to have come to succeed it.'*

Here Cebes joined in and said: 'Goodness yes, Socrates, thank you for reminding me. Several people, you know,
d including Evenus just the other day,* have been asking me about the poems you've made up, putting the tales of Aesop into verse,* and the hymn to Apollo: what had you in mind, they asked, in making them up after you'd come here, when you'd never made up anything before? So if
5 you'd like me to have an answer for Evenus when he asks me again—and I'm quite sure he will—tell me what I should say.'

'Tell him the truth, then, Cebes,' he said: 'I made them, e not because I wanted to compete with him or his verses—I knew that wouldn't be easy—but because I was trying to find out the meaning of certain dreams and fulfil a sacred

duty, in case perhaps it was that kind of art they were
ordering me to make. They were like this, you see: often in   5
my past life the same dream* had visited me, now in one
guise, now in another, but always saying the same thing:
"Socrates," it said, "make art and practise it." Now in
earlier times I used to assume that the dream was urging   61
and telling me to do exactly what I was doing: as people
shout encouragement to runners, so the dream was telling
me to do the very thing that I was doing, to make art, since
philosophy is a very high art form, and that was what I was
making. But now that the trial was over and the festival of   5
the god was preventing my death, I thought that in case it
was art in the popular sense that the dream was command-
ing me to make, I ought not to disobey it, but should make
it; as it was safer not to go off before I'd fulfilled a sacred   b
duty, by making verses and thus obeying the dream. And so
I first made them for the god in whose honour the present
feast was kept. Then, after addressing the god, I reflected
that a poet should, if he were really going to be a poet,
make tales rather than true stories;* and being no teller of   5
tales myself, I therefore used some I had ready to hand; I
knew the tales of Aesop by heart, and I made verses from
the first of those I came across. So give Evenus this
message, Cebes: say goodbye to him, and tell him, if he's   c
sensible, to come after me as quickly as he can. I'm off
today, it seems—by Athenians' orders.'

'What a thing you're urging Evenus to do, Socrates!' said
Simmias. 'I've come across the man often before now; and
from what I've seen of him, he'll hardly be at all willing to   5
obey you.'

'Why,' he said, 'isn't Evenus a philosopher?'

'I believe so,' said Simmias.

'Then Evenus will be willing, and so will everyone who
engages worthily in this business. Perhaps, though, he
won't do violence to himself: they say it's forbidden.' As he   10
said this he lowered his legs to the ground, and then   d
remained sitting in that position for the rest of the
discussion.

Cebes now asked him: 'How can you say this, Socrates?

5

How can it both be forbidden to do violence to oneself, and
5 be the case that the philosopher would be willing to follow
the dying?'

'Why Cebes, haven't you and Simmias heard about such
things through being with Philolaus?'*

'No, nothing definite, Socrates.'

'Well, I myself can speak about them only from hearsay;
10 but what I happen to have heard I don't mind telling you.
e Indeed, maybe it's specially fitting that someone about to
make the journey to the next world should inquire and
speculate as to what we imagine that journey to be like;
after all, what else should one do during the time till
sundown?'

5 'Well then, Socrates, on just what ground do they say it's
forbidden to kill oneself? Because—to answer the question
you were just asking—I certainly did hear from Philolaus,
when he was living with us, and earlier from several others,
that one ought not to do that; but I've never heard
anything definite about it from anyone.'

62 'Well, you must take heart,' he said; 'as maybe you will
hear. Perhaps, though, it will seem surprising to you if this
alone of all rules is unqualified,* and it never happens, as
in other cases, that sometimes and for some people it is
5 better for a person to be dead than alive; and perhaps it
seems surprising to you if those people who would be
better off dead may not without sin do themselves a good
turn, but must await another benefactor.'

Cebes chuckled at this. 'Hark at that, now!' he said,
speaking in his own dialect.

b 'Well yes,' said Socrates, 'it would seem unreasonable,
put that way; but perhaps there is, in fact, some reason for
it. The reason given in mysteries on the subject,* that we
human beings are in some sort of prison,* and that one
5 ought not to release oneself from it or run away, seems to
me a lofty idea and not easy to penetrate; but still, Cebes,
this much seems to me well said: it is gods who care for us,
and for the gods we human beings are among their
belongings. Don't you think so?'

10 'I do,' said Cebes.

'Well, if one of your belongings were to kill itself,   c
without your signifying that you wanted it to die, wouldn't
you be vexed with it, and punish it, if you had any
punishment at hand?'

'Certainly.'   5

'So perhaps, in that case, it isn't unreasonable that one
should not kill oneself until God sends some necessity, such
as the one now before us.'

'Yes, that does seem fair,' said Cebes. 'But then what you
were saying just now—that philosophers should be willing   10
to die lightly—that seems odd, if what we were just saying, d
that it is God who cares for us, and that we are his
belongings, is well founded. Because it's unreasonable that
the wisest people should not be resentful at quitting this   5
service, where they're directed by the best directors there
are—the gods; since someone of that sort, surely, doesn't
believe he'll care for himself any better on becoming free. A
stupid person would perhaps believe that: he would think
he should escape from his master, and wouldn't reflect that   e
a good master is not one to escape from, but to stay with as
long as possible, and so his escape would be irrational; but
anyone with intelligence would surely always want to be
with one better than himself. Yet in that case, Socrates, the
very opposite of what was said just now seems likely: it's   5
the wise who should be resentful at dying, whereas the
foolish should welcome it.'

When Socrates heard this he seemed to me pleased at
Cebes' persistence, and looking at us he said: 'There goes   63
Cebes, always hunting down arguments, and not at all
willing to accept at once what anyone may say.'

'Well yes,' said Simmias; 'but this time, Socrates, I think
myself there's something in what Cebes says: why, indeed,
should truly wise men want to escape from masters who
are better than themselves, and be separated from them
lightly? So I think it's at you that Cebes is aiming his
argument, because you take so lightly your leaving both
ourselves and the gods, who are good rulers by your own
admission.'

'What you both say is fair,' he said; 'as I take you to   b mean that I should defend myself against these charges as if in a court of law.'

'Yes, exactly,' said Simmias.

'Very well then,' he said; 'let me try to defend myself
5 more convincingly before you than I did before the jury. Because if I didn't believe, Simmias and Cebes, that I shall enter the presence, first, of other gods both wise and good, and next of dead people better than those in this world, then I should be wrong not to be resentful at death; but as
c it is, be assured that I expect to join the company of good men—although that point I shouldn't affirm with absolute conviction; but I shall enter the presence of gods who are very good masters, be assured that if there's anything I should affirm on such matters, it is that. So that's why I am
5 not so resentful, but rather am hopeful that there is something in store for those who've died—in fact, as we've long been told, something far better for the good than for the wicked.'

'Well then, Socrates,' said Simmias, 'do you mean to go off keeping this thought to yourself, or would you share it
d with us too? We have a common claim on this benefit as well, I think; and at the same time your defence will be made, if you persuade us of what you say.'

'All right, I'll try,' he said. 'But first let's find out what it is that Crito here has been wanting to say, for some time past, I think.'

5 'Why Socrates,' said Crito, 'it's simply that the man who's going to give you the poison has been telling me for some time that you must be warned to talk as little as possible: he says people get heated through talking too
e much, and one must bring nothing of that sort in contact with the poison;* people doing that sort of thing are sometimes obliged, otherwise, to drink twice or even three times.'

'Never mind him,' said Socrates. 'Just let him prepare
5 his stuff so as to give two doses, or even three if need be.'

'Yes, I pretty well knew it,' said Crito; 'but he's been giving me trouble for some while.'

'Let him be,' he said. 'Now then, with you for my jury I want to give my defence, and show with what good reason, as it seems to me, a man who has truly spent his life in philosophy feels confident when about to die, and is hopeful that, when he has died, he will win very great benefits in the other world. So I'll try, Simmias and Cebes, to explain how this could be.

'Other people may well be unaware that all who actually engage in philosophy aright are practising nothing other than dying and being dead.* Now if this is true, it would be odd indeed for them to be eager in their whole life for nothing but that, and yet to be resentful when it comes, the very thing they'd long been eager for and practised.'

Simmias laughed at this and said: 'Goodness, Socrates, you've made me laugh, even though I wasn't much inclined to laugh just now. I imagine that most people, on hearing that, would think it very well said of philosophers—and our own countrymen would quite agree—*that they are, indeed, longing for death, and that they, at any rate, are well aware that that is what philosophers deserve to undergo.'

'Yes, and what they say would be true, Simmias, except for their claim to be aware of it themselves; because they aren't aware in what sense genuine philosophers are longing for death and deserving of it, and what kind of death they deserve. Anyway, let's discuss it among ourselves, disregarding them: do we suppose that death is a reality?'

'Certainly,' rejoined Simmias.

'And that it is nothing but the separation of the soul from the body?* And that being dead is this: the body's having come to be apart, separated from the soul, alone by itself, and the soul's being apart, alone by itself, separated from the body? Death can't be anything else but that, can it?'

'No, it's just that.'

'Now look, my friend, and see if maybe you agree with me on these points; because through them I think we'll improve our knowledge of what we're examining. Do you

9

think it befits a philosophical man to be keen about the so-called pleasures of, for example, food and drink?'

5 'Not in the least, Socrates,' said Simmias.

'And what about those of sex?'

'Not at all.'

'And what about the other services to the body? Do you think such a person regards them as of any value? For 10 instance, the possession of smart clothes and shoes, and the other bodily adornments—do you think he values them e highly, or does he disdain them, except in so far as he's absolutely compelled to share in them?'

'I think the genuine philosopher disdains them.'

'Do you think in general, then, that such a person's 5 concern is not for the body, but so far as he can stand aside from it, is directed towards the soul?'

'I do.'

'Then is it clear that, first, in such matters as those the 65 philosopher differs from other people in releasing his soul, as far as possible, from its communion with the body?'

'It appears so.'

'And presumably, Simmias, it does seem to most people 5 that someone who finds nothing of that sort pleasant, and takes no part in those things, doesn't deserve to live; rather, one who cares nothing for the pleasures that come by way of the body runs pretty close to being dead.'

'Yes, what you say is quite true.'

10 'And now, what about the actual gaining of wisdom? Is b the body a hindrance or not, if one enlists it as a partner in the quest? This is the sort of thing I mean: do sight and hearing afford mankind any truth, or aren't even the poets always harping on such themes, telling us that we neither 5 hear nor see anything accurately?* And yet if those of all the bodily senses are neither accurate nor clear, the others will hardly be so; because they are, surely, all inferior to those. Don't you think so?'

'Certainly.'

'So when does the soul attain the truth?* Because 10 plainly, whenever it sets about examining anything in company with the body, it is completely taken in by it.'

10

'That's true.'   c

'So isn't it in reasoning, if anywhere at all, that any realities become manifest to it?'

'Yes.'

'And it reasons best, presumably, whenever none of   5
these things bothers it, neither hearing nor sight nor pain, nor any pleasure either, but whenever it comes to be alone by itself as far as possible, disregarding the body, and whenever, having the least possible communion and contact with it, it strives for reality.'

'That is so.'   10

'So there again the soul of the philosopher utterly disdains the body and flees from it, seeking rather to come   d
to be alone by itself?'

'It seems so.'

'Well now, what about things of this sort, Simmias? Do we say that a just itself is a reality or not?'   5

'Yes, we most certainly do!'

'And likewise, a beautiful and a good?'*

'Of course.'

'Now did you ever yet see any such things with your eyes?'

'Certainly not.'   10

'Well did you grasp them with any other bodily sense-perception? And I'm talking about them all—about largeness, health, and strength, for example—and, in short, about the being of all other such things, what each one   e
actually is; is it through the body that the truest view of them is gained, or isn't it rather thus: whoever of us is prepared to think most fully and minutely of each object of his inquiry, in itself, will come closest to the knowledge of each?'   5

'Yes, certainly.'

'Then would that be achieved most purely by one who approached each object with his intellect alone as far as possible, neither applying sight in his thinking, nor dragging in any other sense to accompany his reasoning;   66
rather, using his intellect alone by itself and unsullied, he would undertake the hunt for each reality alone by itself

and unsullied; he would be separated as far as possible
5 from his eyes and ears, and virtually from his whole body,
on the ground that it confuses the soul, and doesn't allow it
to gain truth and wisdom when in partnership with it: isn't
this the one, Simmias, who will attain reality, if anyone
will?'

10   'What you say is abundantly true, Socrates,' said
Simmias.

b   'For all those reasons, then, some such view as this must
present itself to genuine philosophers, so that they say such
things to one another as these: "There now, it looks as if
some sort of track is leading us, together with our reason,
5 astray in our inquiry: as long as we possess the body, and
our soul is contaminated by such an evil, we'll surely never
adequately gain what we desire—and that, we say, is truth.
Because the body affords us countless distractions, owing
c to the nurture it must have; and again, if any illnesses befall
it, they hamper our pursuit of reality. Besides, it fills us up
with lusts and desires, with fears and fantasies of every
kind, and with any amount of trash, so that really and truly
5 we are, as the saying goes,* never able to think of anything
at all because of it. Thus, it's nothing but the body and its
desires that brings wars and factions and fighting; because
d it's over the gaining of wealth that all wars take place, and
we're compelled to gain wealth because of the body,
enslaved as we are to its service; so for all those reasons it
leaves us no leisure for philosophy. And the worst of it all is
5 that if we do get any leisure from it, and turn to some
inquiry, once again it intrudes everywhere in our researches,
setting up a clamour and disturbance, and striking terror,
so that the truth can't be discerned because of it. Well now,
it really has been shown us that if we're ever going to know
e anything purely, we must be rid of it, and must view the
objects themselves with the soul by itself; it's then,
apparently, that the thing we desire and whose lovers we
claim to be, wisdom, will be ours—when we have died, as
the argument indicates, though not while we live. Because,
5 if we can know nothing purely in the body's company, then
one of two things must be true: either knowledge is

nowhere to be gained, or else it is for the dead; since then, but no sooner, will the soul be alone by itself apart from   67 the body. And therefore while we live, it would seem that we shall be closest to knowledge in this way—if we consort with the body as little as possible, and do not commune with it, except in so far as we must, and do not infect   5 ourselves with its nature, but remain pure from it, until God himself shall release us; and being thus pure, through separation from the body's folly, we shall probably be in like company, and shall know through our own selves all   b that is unsullied—and that, I dare say, is what the truth is; because never will it be permissible for impure to touch pure." Such are the things, I think, Simmias, that all who are rightly called lovers of knowledge must say to one another, and must believe. Don't you agree?'   5

'Emphatically, Socrates.'

'Well then, if that's true, my friend,' said Socrates, 'there's plenty of hope for one who arrives where I'm going, that there, if anywhere, he will adequately possess the object that's been our great concern in life gone by; and   10 thus the journey now appointed for me may also be made   c with good hope by any other man who regards his intellect as prepared, by having been, in a manner, purified.'

'Yes indeed,' said Simmias.

'Then doesn't purification turn out to be just what's been   5 mentioned for some while in our discussion—the parting of the soul from the body as far as possible, and the habituating of it to assemble and gather itself together, away from every part of the body, alone by itself, and to live, so far as it can, both in the present and in the hereafter,   d released from the body, as from fetters?'

'Yes indeed.'

'And is it just this that is named "death"—a release and parting of soul from body?'   5

'Indeed it is.'

'And it's especially those who practise philosophy aright, or rather they alone, who are always eager to release it, as we say, and the occupation of philosophers is just this, isn't it—a release and parting of soul from body?'   10

'It seems so.'

'Then wouldn't it be absurd, as I said at the start, for a
e man to prepare himself in his life to live as close as he can
to being dead, and then to be resentful when that comes to
him?'

'It would be absurd, of course.'

'Truly then, Simmias, those who practise philosophy
5 aright are cultivating dying, and for them, least of all men,
does being dead hold any terror. Look at it like this: if
they've set themselves at odds with the body at every point,
and desire to possess their soul alone by itself, wouldn't it
68 be quite illogical if they were afraid and resentful when that
came about—if, that is, they didn't go gladly to the place
where, on arrival, they may hope to attain what they
longed for throughout life, namely wisdom—and to be rid
of the company of that with which they'd set themselves at
5 odds? Or again, many have been willing to enter Hades of
their own accord, in quest of human loves, of wives and
sons* who have died, led by this hope, that there they
would see and be united with those they desired; will
anyone, then, who truly longs for wisdom, and who firmly
b holds this same hope, that nowhere but in Hades will he
attain it in any way worth mentioning, be resentful at
dying; and will he not go there gladly? One must suppose
so, my friend, if he's truly a lover of wisdom;* since this
will be his firm belief, that nowhere else but there will he
5 attain wisdom purely. Yet if that is so, wouldn't it, as I said
just now, be quite illogical if such a person were afraid of
death?'

'Yes, quite illogical!'

'Then if you see a man resentful that he is going to die,
c isn't that proof enough for you that he's no lover of
wisdom after all, but what we may call a lover of the body?
And this same man turns out, in some sense, to be a lover
of riches and of prestige, either one of those or both.'

'It's just as you say.'

5 'Well now, Simmias, isn't it also true that what is named
"bravery"* belongs especially to people of the disposition
we have described?'

'Most certainly.'

'And then temperance too, even what most people name "temperance"—not being excited over one's desires, but being scornful of them and well-ordered—belongs, doesn't it, only to those who utterly scorn the body and live in love of wisdom?'   10

'It must.'   d

'Yes, because if you care to consider the bravery and temperance of other people, you'll find it strange.'

'How so, Socrates?'

'You know, don't you, that all others count death among great evils?'   5

'Very much so.'

'Is it, then, through being afraid of greater evils that the brave among them abide death, whenever they do so?'

'It is.'   10

'Then, it's through fearing and fear that all except philosophers are brave; and yet it's surely illogical that anyone should be brave through fear and cowardice.'*

'It certainly is.'   e

'And what about those of them who are well-ordered? Aren't they in this same state, temperate through a kind of intemperance? True, we say that's impossible; but still that state of simple-minded temperance does turn out in their case to be like this: it's because they're afraid of being deprived of further pleasures, and desire them, that they abstain from some because they're overcome by others. True, they call it "intemperance" to be ruled by pleasures, but still that's what happens to them: they overcome some pleasures because they're overcome by others. And that is the sort of thing that was just mentioned: after a fashion, they achieve temperance because of intemperance.'   69

'Yes, so it seems.'   5

'Yes, Simmias, my good friend; since this may not be the right exchange with a view to goodness, the exchanging of pleasures for pleasures, pains for pains, and fear for fear, greater or lesser ones, like coins; it may be, rather, that this alone is the right coin, for which one should exchange all those things—wisdom; and the buying and selling of all   10   b

15

things for that, or rather with that, may be real bravery,
temperance, justice, and, in short, true goodness in
company with wisdom,* whether pleasures and fears and
5 all else of that sort be added or taken away; but as for their
being parted from wisdom and exchanged for one another,
goodness of that sort may be a kind of illusory façade, and
fit for slaves indeed, and may have nothing healthy or true
c about it; whereas, truth to tell, temperance, justice, and
bravery may in fact be a kind of purification of all such
things, and wisdom itself a kind of purifying rite. So it
really looks as if those who established our initiations are
5 no mean people, but have in fact long been saying in riddles
that whoever arrives in Hades unadmitted to the rites, and
uninitiated, shall lie in the slough,* while one who arrives
there purified and initiated shall dwell with gods. For truly
there are, so say those concerned with the initiations,
d "many who bear the wand, but few who are devotees".*
Now these latter, in my view, are none other than those
who have practised philosophy aright. And it's to be
among them that I myself have striven, in every way I
5 could, neglecting nothing during my life within my power.
Whether I have striven aright and we have achieved
anything, we shall, I think, know for certain, God willing,
in a little while, on arrival yonder.

'There's my defence, then, Simmias and Cebes, to show
e how reasonable it is for me not to take it hard or be
resentful at leaving you and my masters here, since I believe
that there also, no less than here, I shall find good masters
and companions; so if I'm any more convincing in my
5 defence to you than to the Athenian jury, it would be well.'

When Socrates had said that, Cebes rejoined: 'The other
things you say, Socrates, I find excellent; but what you say
70 about the soul is the subject of much disbelief: people fear
that when it's been separated from the body, it may no
longer exist anywhere, but that on the very day a person
dies, it may be destroyed and perish, as soon as it's
separated from the body; and that as it goes out, it may be
5 dispersed like breath or smoke, go flying off, and exist no

longer anywhere at all. True, if it did exist somewhere, gathered together alone by itself, and separated from those evils you were recounting just now, there'd be plenty of hope, Socrates, and a fine hope it would be, that what you **b** say is true; but on just this point, perhaps, one needs no little reassuring and convincing, that when the person has died, his soul exists, and that it possesses some power and wisdom.'

'That's true, Cebes,' said Socrates; 'but then what are we **5** to do? Would you like us to speculate* on those very questions, and see whether that is likely to be the case or not?'

'For my part anyway,' said Cebes, 'I'd gladly hear whatever opinion you have about them.'

'Well,' said Socrates, 'I really don't think anyone **10** listening now, even if he were a comic poet,* would say **c** that I'm talking idly, and arguing about things that don't concern me. If you agree, then, we should look into the matter.

'Let's consider it, perhaps, in this way: do the souls of human beings exist in Hades when they have died, or do **5** they not? Now there's an ancient doctrine, which we've recalled,* that they do exist in that world, entering it from this one, and that they re-enter this world and are born again from the dead; yet if that is so, if living people are born again from those who have died, surely our souls would have to exist in that world? Because they could **d** hardly be born again, if they didn't exist; so it would be sufficient evidence for the truth of those claims, if it really became plain that living people are born from the dead and from nowhere else; but if that isn't so, some other argument would be needed.' **5**

'Certainly,' said Cebes.

'Well now, consider the matter, if you want to understand more readily, in connection not only with mankind, but with all animals and plants; and, in general, for all things subject to coming-to-be,* let's see whether everything **e** comes to be in this way: opposites come to be only from their opposites—in the case of all things that actually have

an opposite—as, for example, the beautiful is opposite, of course, to the ugly,* just to unjust, and so on in countless other cases. So let's consider this: is it necessary that
5 whatever has an opposite comes to be only from its opposite? For example, when a thing comes to be larger, it must, surely, come to be larger from being smaller before?'

'Yes.'

10 'And again, if it comes to be smaller, it will come to be
71 smaller later from being larger before?'

'That's so.'

'And that which is weaker comes to be, presumably, from a stronger, and that which is faster from a slower?'

5 'Certainly.'

'And again, if a thing comes to be worse, it's from a better, and if more just, from a more unjust?'

'Of course.'

'Are we satisfied, then, that all things come to be in this
10 way, opposite things from opposites?'

'Certainly.'

'Now again, do those things have a further feature of this sort: between the members of every pair of opposites, since they are two, aren't there two processes of coming-to-be,
b from one to the other, and back again from the latter to the former? Thus, between a larger thing and a smaller, isn't there increase and decrease, so that in the one case we speak of "increasing" and in the other of "decreasing"?'

5 'Yes.'

'And similarly with separating and combining, cooling and heating, and all such; even if in some cases we don't use the names,* still in actual fact mustn't the same principle everywhere hold good: they come to be from each
10 other, and there's a process of coming-to-be of each into the other?'

'Certainly.'

c 'Well then, is there an opposite to living, as sleeping is opposite to being awake?'

'Certainly.'

'What is it?'

5 'Being dead.'

18

'Then those come to be from each other, if they are opposites; and between the pair of them, since they are two, the processes of coming-to-be are two?'

'Of course.'

'Now then,' said Socrates, 'I'll tell you one of the couples I was just mentioning, the couple itself and its processes; and you tell me the other. My couple is sleeping and being awake: being awake comes to be from sleeping, and sleeping from being awake, and their processes are going to sleep and waking up. Is that sufficient for you or not?'

'Certainly.'

'Now it's for you to tell me in the same way about life and death. You say, don't you, that being dead is opposite to living?'

'I do.'

'And that they come to be from each other?'

'Yes.'

'Then what is it that comes to be from that which is living?'

'That which is dead.'

'And what comes to be from that which is dead?'

'I must admit that it's that which is living.'

'Then it's from those that are dead, Cebes, that living things and living people are born?'

'Apparently.'

'Then our souls do exist in Hades.'

'So it seems.'

'Now *one* of the relevant processes here is obvious, isn't it? For dying is obvious enough, surely?'

'It certainly is.'

'What shall we do then? Shan't we assign the opposite process to balance it? Will nature be lame in this respect? Or must we supply some process opposite to dying?'

'We surely must.'

'What will this be?'

'Coming to life again.'

'Then if there *is* such a thing as coming to life again, wouldn't this, coming to life again, be a process from dead to living people?'

'Certainly.'

'In that way too, then, we're agreed that living people are
5 born from the dead no less than dead people from the
living; and we thought that, if that were the case, it would
be sufficient evidence that the souls of the dead must exist
somewhere, whence they are born again.'

10 'I think, Socrates, that that must follow from our
admissions.'

'Then look at it this way,* Cebes, and you'll see, I think,
that our admissions were not mistaken. If there were not
b perpetual reciprocity in coming to be, between one set of
things and another, revolving in a circle, as it were—if,
instead, coming-to-be were a linear process from one thing
into its opposite only, without any bending back in the
other direction or reversal, do you realize that all things
5 would ultimately have the same form: the same fate would
overtake them, and they would cease from coming to be?'

'What do you mean?'

'It's not at all hard to understand what I mean. If, for
example, there were such a thing as going to sleep, but
from sleeping there were no reverse process of waking up,
c you realize that everything would ultimately make
Endymion* seem a mere trifle: he'd be nowhere, because
the same fate as his, sleeping, would have overtaken
everything else. Again, if everything were combined, but
not separated, then Anaxagoras' notion of "all things
5 together" would soon be realized.* And similarly, my dear
Cebes, if all things that partake in life were to die, but when
they'd died, the dead remained in that form, and didn't
come back to life, wouldn't it be quite inevitable that
d everything would ultimately be dead, and nothing would
live? Because if the living things came to be from the other
things,* but the living things were to die, what could
possibly prevent everything from being completely spent in
being dead?'

'Nothing whatever, in my view, Socrates,' said Cebes;
5 'what you say seems to be perfectly true.'

'Yes, it certainly is true, Cebes, as I see it; and we're not
deceived in making just those admissions: there really is

such a thing as coming to life again, living people *are* born
from the dead, and the souls of the dead exist.'   e

'Yes, and besides, Socrates,' Cebes replied, 'there's also
that theory you're always putting forward, that our   5
learning is actually nothing but recollection;* according to
that too, if it's true, what we are now reminded of we must
have learned at some former time. But that would be   73
impossible, unless our souls existed somewhere before
being born in this human form; so in this way too, it
appears that the soul is something immortal.'*

'Yes, what are the proofs of those points, Cebes?' put in
Simmias. 'Remind me, as I don't recall them very well at   5
the moment.'

'One excellent argument,' said Cebes, 'is that when
people are questioned, and if the questions are well put,
they state the truth about everything for themselves—* and
yet unless knowledge and a correct account were present   10
within them, they'd be unable to do that; thus, if one takes   b
them to diagrams or anything else of that sort, one has
there the plainest evidence that that is so.'

'But if that doesn't convince you, Simmias,' said Socrates,
'then see whether maybe you agree if you look at it this
way. Apparently you doubt whether what is called   5
"learning" is recollection?'

'I don't doubt it,' said Simmias; 'but I do need to
undergo just what the argument is about, to be "reminded".
Actually, from the way Cebes set about stating it, I do
almost recall it and am nearly convinced; but I'd like, none
the less, to hear now how you set about stating it yourself.'   10

'I'll put it this way. We agree, I take it, that if anyone is   c
to be reminded of a thing, he must have known that thing
at some time previously.'

'Certainly.'

'Then do we also agree on this point: that whenever
knowledge comes to be present in this sort of way, it is   5
recollection? I mean in some such way as this: if someone,
on seeing a thing, or hearing it, or getting any other sense-
perception of it, not only recognizes that thing, but also

21

thinks of something else, which is the object not of the same knowledge but of another, don't we then rightly say

b that he's been "reminded" of the object of which he has got the thought?'

'What do you mean?'

'Take the following examples: knowledge of a person, surely, is other than that of a lyre?'

'Of course.'

5 'Well now, you know what happens to lovers, whenever they see a lyre or cloak or anything else their loves are accustomed to use: they recognize the lyre, and they get in their mind, don't they, the form of the boy whose lyre it is? And that is recollection. Likewise, someone seeing Simmias

10 is often reminded of Cebes,* and there'd surely be countless other such cases.'

'Countless indeed!' said Simmias.

e 'Then is something of that sort a kind of recollection? More especially, though, whenever it happens to someone in connection with things he's since forgotten, through lapse of time or inattention?'

'Certainly.'

5 'Again now, is it possible, on seeing a horse depicted or a lyre depicted, to be reminded of a person; and on seeing Simmias depicted, to be reminded of Cebes?'

'Certainly.'

'And also, on seeing Simmias depicted, to be reminded of

10 Simmias himself?'

74 'Yes, that's possible.'

'In all those cases, then, doesn't it turn out that there is recollection from similar things, but also from dissimilar things?'

'It does.'

'But whenever one is reminded of something from

5 similar things, mustn't one experience something further: mustn't one think whether or not the thing is lacking at all, in its similarity, in relation to what one is reminded of?'

'One must.'

'Then consider whether this is the case. We say, don't

10 we, that there is something that is equal—*I don't mean a

log to a log, or a stone to a stone, or anything else of that sort, but some further thing beyond all those, the equal itself: are we to say that it is a reality or not?'

'We most certainly are to say that it is,' said Simmias; **b** 'unquestionably!'

'And do we know it, know what it is?'

'Certainly.'

'Where did we get the knowledge of it? Wasn't it from the things we were just mentioning: on seeing logs or 5 stones or other equal things, wasn't it from those that we thought of that object, it being different from them? Or doesn't it seem different to you? Look at it this way: aren't equal stones and logs, the very same ones, sometimes evidently* equal to one, but not to another?'*

'Yes, certainly.' 10

'But now, were the equals themselves* ever, in your **c** view, evidently unequal, or equality inequality?'

'Never yet, Socrates.'

'Then those equals, and the equal itself, are not the 5 same.'

'By no means, Socrates, in my view.'

'But still, it is from those equals, different as they are from that equal, that you have thought of and got the knowledge of it?'

'That's perfectly true.' 10

'It being either similar to them or dissimilar?'

'Certainly.'

'Anyway, it makes no difference; so long as on seeing one thing, one does, from that sight, think of another, **d** whether it be similar or dissimilar, that must be recollection.'

'Certainly.'

'Well now, with regard to the instances in the logs, and, in general, the equals we mentioned just now, are we 5 affected in some way as this: do they seem to us to be equal in the same way as is the thing itself, that which it is? Do they fall short of it at all in being like the equal, or not?'

'Very far short of it.'

'Then whenever anyone, on seeing a thing, thinks to

23

10 himself, "this thing that I now see seeks to be like another
e reality, but falls short, and cannot be like that object: it is
inferior", do we agree that the man who thinks that must
previously have known the object he says it resembles but
falls short of?'

5 'He must.'

'Now then, have we ourselves been affected in just that
way, or not, with regard to the equals and the equal itself?'

'Indeed we have.'

'Then we must previously have known the equal, before
75 that time when we first, on seeing the equals, thought that
all of them were striving to be like the equal* but fell short
of it.'

'That is so.'

5 'Yet we also agree on this: we haven't derived the
thought of it, nor could we do so, from anywhere but
seeing or touching or some other of the senses—I'm
counting all those as the same.'

'Yes, they are the same, Socrates, for what the argument
10 seeks to show.'

'But of course it is from one's sense-perceptions that one
b must think that all sensible items are striving for that thing
which equal is, yet are inferior to it; or how shall we put
it?'

'Like that.'

'Then it must, surely, have been before we began to see
5 and hear and use the other senses that we got knowledge of
the equal itself, of what it is, if we were going to refer the
equals from our sense-perceptions to it, supposing that all
things are doing their best to be like it, but are inferior to
it.'

'That must follow from what's been said before,
Socrates.'

10 'Now we were seeing and hearing, and were possessed of
our other senses, weren't we, just as soon as we were
born?'

'Certainly.'

c 'But we must, we're saying, have got our knowledge of
the equal before those?'

'Yes.'

'Then it seems that we must have got it before we were   5
born.'

'It seems so.'

'Now if, having got it before birth, we were born in
possession of it, did we know, both before birth and as
soon as we were born, not only the equal, the larger and   10
the smaller, but everything of that sort? Because our
present argument concerns the beautiful itself, and the   d
good itself, and just and holy, no less than the equal; in
fact, as I say, it concerns everything on which we set this
seal, "that which it is",* in the questions we ask and in the
answers we give. And so we must have got pieces of   5
knowledge of all those things before birth.'

'That is so.'

'Moreover, if having got them, we did not on each
occasion forget them, we must always be born knowing,
and must continue to know throughout life: because this is
knowing—to possess knowledge one has got of something,   10
and not to have lost it; or isn't loss of knowledge what we
mean by "forgetting", Simmias?'

'Certainly it is, Socrates.'   e

'But on the other hand, I suppose that if, having got them
before birth, we lost them on being born, and later on,
using the senses about the things in question, we regain
those pieces of knowledge that we possessed at some
former time, in that case wouldn't what we call "learning"   5
be the regaining of knowledge belonging to us? And in
saying that that was being reminded, shouldn't we be
speaking correctly?'

'Certainly.'

'Yes, because it did seem possible, on sensing an object,   76
whether by seeing or hearing or getting some other sense-
perception of it, to think from that of some other thing one
had forgotten—either a thing to which the object, though
dissimilar to it, was related, or else something to which it
was similar; so, as I say, one of two things is true: either all   5
of us were born knowing those objects, and we know them
throughout life; or those we speak of as "learning" are

simply being reminded later on, and learning would be recollection.'

'That's quite true, Socrates.'

'Then which do you choose, Simmias? That we are born

b knowing, or that we are later reminded of the things we'd gained knowledge of before?'

'At the moment, Socrates, I can't make a choice.'

'Well, can you make one on the following point, and

5 what do you think about it? If a man knows things, can he give an account of what he knows or not?'

'Of course he can, Socrates.'

'And do you think everyone can give an account of those objects we were discussing just now?'

10 'I only wish they could,' said Simmias; 'but I'm afraid that, on the contrary, this time tomorrow there may no longer be any human being who can do so properly.'

c 'You don't then, Simmias, think that everyone knows those objects?'

'By no means.'

'Are they, then, reminded of what they once learned?'

5 'They must be.'

'When did our souls get the knowledge of those objects? Not, at any rate, since we were born as human beings.'

'Indeed not.'

'Earlier, then.'

10 'Yes.'

'Then our souls did exist earlier, Simmias, before entering human form, apart from bodies; and they possessed wisdom.'

'Unless maybe, Socrates, we get those pieces of know-

15 ledge at the very moment of birth; that time still remains.'

d 'Very well, my friend; but then at what other time, may I ask, do we lose them? We aren't born with them, as we agreed just now. Do we then lose them at the very time at which we get them? Or have you any other time to suggest?'

5 'None at all, Socrates. I didn't realize I was talking nonsense.'

'Then is our position as follows, Simmias? If the objects we're always harping on exist, a beautiful, and a good, and all such reality, and if we refer all the things from our sense-perceptions to that reality, finding again what was   e
formerly ours,* and if we compare these things with that, then just as surely as those objects exist, so also must our souls exist* before we are born. On the other hand, if they don't exist, this argument will have gone for nothing. Is this the position? Is it equally necessary that those objects   5
exist, and that our souls existed before birth, and if the former don't exist, then neither did the latter?'

'It's abundantly clear to me, Socrates,' said Simmias, 'that there's the same necessity in either case, and the argument takes opportune refuge in the view that our souls   77
exist before birth, just as surely as the reality of which you're now speaking. Because I myself find nothing so plain to me as that all such objects, beautiful and good and all the others you were speaking of just now, have the fullest possible reality; so in my view it's been adequately   5
proved.'

'And what about Cebes?' said Socrates. 'We must convince Cebes too.'

'It's adequate for him, I think,' said Simmias; 'though he's the most obstinate of people when it comes to doubting arguments. But I think he's been sufficiently convinced that our souls existed before we were born. Whether they will still exist, however, after we've died,   b
doesn't seem, even to me, to have been shown, Socrates; but the point Cebes made just now still stands—the popular fear that when a human being dies, his soul may be dispersed at that time, and that that may be the end of its   5
existence. Because what's to prevent it from coming to be and being put together from some other source, and from existing before it enters a human body, yet when it has entered one, and again been separated from it, from then meeting its end, and being itself destroyed?'

'You're right, Simmias,' said Cebes. 'It seems that half,   c
as it were, of what is needed has been shown—that our souls existed before we were born; it must also be shown

that they will exist after we've died, no less than before we
5 were born, if the proof is going to be complete.'

'That's been proved already, Simmias and Cebes,' said
Socrates, 'if you will combine this argument with the one
we agreed on earlier, to the effect that all that is living
d comes from that which is dead. Because if the soul does
have previous existence, and if when it enters upon living
and being born, it must come from no other source than
death and being dead, surely it must also exist after it has
died, given that it has to be born again? So your point has
5 been proved already. But even so, I think you and Simmias
would like to thrash out this argument still further; you
seem afraid, like children, that as the soul goes out from the
e body, the wind may literally blow it apart and disperse it,
especially when someone happens not to die in calm
weather but in a high wind.'

Cebes laughed at this, and said: 'Try to reassure us,
Socrates, as if we were afraid; or rather, not as if we were
5 afraid ourselves—but maybe there's a child inside us, who
has fears of that sort. Try to persuade him, then, to stop
being afraid of death, as if it were a bogeyman.'

'Well, you must sing spells to him every day,' said
Socrates, 'till you've charmed it out of him.'

78 'And where', he said, 'shall we find a charmer for such
fears, Socrates, now that you're leaving us?'

'Greece is a large country, Cebes, which has good men in
it, I suppose; and there are many foreign races too. You
5 must ransack all of them in search of such a charmer,
sparing neither money nor trouble, because there's no
object on which you could more opportunely spend your
money. And you yourselves must search too, along with
one another; you may not easily find anyone more capable
of doing that than yourselves.'

10 'That shall certainly be done,' said Cebes; 'but let's go
b back to the point where we left off, if you've no objection.'

'Of course not; why should I?'

'Good.'

'Well then,' said Socrates, 'mustn't we ask ourselves

28

something like this: What kind of thing is liable to undergo 5
this fate—namely, dispersal—and for what kind of thing
should we fear lest it undergo it? And what kind of thing is
not liable to it? And next, mustn't we further ask to which
of those two kinds soul belongs, and then feel either
confidence or fear for our own soul accordingly?'

'That's true.' 10

'Then is it true that what has been put together and is c
naturally composite is liable to undergo this, to break up at
the point at which it was put together; whereas if there be
anything non-composite, it alone is liable, if anything is, to
escape this?'

'That's what I think,' said Cebes. 5

'Well now, aren't the things that are constant and
unvarying most likely to be the non-composite, whereas
things that vary and are never constant are likely to be
composite?'

'I think so.'

'Then let's go back to those entities to which we turned 10
in our earlier argument. Is the reality itself, whose being we d
give an account of in asking and answering questions,*
unvarying and constant, or does it vary? Does the equal
itself, the beautiful itself, that which each thing itself is, the
real, ever admit of any change whatever? Or does that 5
which each of them is, being uniform alone by itself,
remain unvarying and constant, and never admit of any
kind of alteration in any way or respect whatever?'

'It must be unvarying and constant, Socrates,' said
Cebes.

'But what about the many beautiful things, such as 10
human beings or horses or cloaks or anything else at all of e
that kind? Or equals, or all things that bear the same name
as those objects? Are they constant, or are they just the
opposite of those others, and practically never constant
at all, either in relation to themselves or to one
another?'

'That is their condition,' said Cebes; 'they are never 5
unvarying.'

'Now these things you could actually touch and see and 79

sense with the other senses, couldn't you, whereas those
that are constant you could lay hold of only by reasoning
of the intellect; aren't such things, rather, invisible and not
seen?'

5   'What you say is perfectly true.'

'Then would you like us to posit two kinds of beings, the
one kind seen, the other invisible?'

'Let's posit them.'

'And the invisible is always constant, whereas the seen is
10 never constant?'

'Let's posit that too.'

b   'Well, but we ourselves are part body and part soul,*
aren't we?'

'We are.'

'Then to which kind do we say that the body will be
5 more similar and more akin?'

'That's clear to anyone: obviously to the seen.'

'And what about the soul? Is it seen or invisible?'

'It's not seen by human beings, at any rate, Socrates.'

'But we meant, surely, things seen and not seen with
10 reference to human nature; or do you think we meant any
other?'

'We meant human nature.'

'What do we say about soul, then? Is it seen or unseen?'

'It's not seen.'

'Then it's invisible?'

15 'Yes.'

'Then soul is more similar than body to the invisible,
whereas body is more similar to that which is seen.'

c   'That must be so, Socrates.'

'Now weren't we saying a while ago that whenever the
soul uses the body as a means to study anything, either by
seeing or hearing or any other sense—because to use the
5 body as a means is to study a thing through sense-
perception—then it is dragged by the body towards objects
that are never constant; and it wanders about itself, and is
confused and dizzy, as if drunk, by virtue of contact with
things of a similar kind?'

'Certainly.'

'Whereas whenever it studies alone by itself, it departs   d
yonder towards that which is pure and always existent and
immortal and unvarying, and by virtue of its kinship with
it, enters always into its company, whenever it has come to
be alone by itself, and whenever it may do so; then it has   5
ceased from its wandering and, when it is about those
objects, it is always constant and unvarying, because of its
contact with things of a similar kind; and this condition of
it is called "wisdom", is it not?'

'That's very well said and perfectly true, Socrates.'

'Once again, then, in the light of our earlier and present
arguments, to which kind do you think that soul is more   e
similar and more akin?'

'Everyone, I think, Socrates, even the slowest learner,
following this line of inquiry, would agree that soul is
totally and altogether more similar to what is unvarying   5
than to what is not.'

'And what about the body?'

'That is more like the latter.'

'Now look at it this way too: when soul and body are
present in the same thing, nature ordains that the one shall   80
serve and be ruled, whereas the other shall rule and be
master; here again, which do you think is similar to the
divine and which to the mortal? Don't you think the divine
is naturally adapted for ruling and domination, whereas   5
the mortal is adapted for being ruled and for service?'

'I do.'

'Which kind, then, does the soul resemble?'

'Obviously, Socrates, the soul resembles the divine, and
the body the mortal.'

'Consider, then, Cebes, if these are our conclusions from   10
all that's been said: soul is most similar to what is divine,   b
immortal, intelligible, uniform, indissoluble, unvarying,
and constant in relation to itself; whereas body, in its turn,
is most similar to what is human, mortal, multiform, non-
intelligible, dissoluble, and never constant in relation to   5
itself. Have we anything to say against those statements,
my dear Cebes, to show that they're false?'

'We haven't.'

31

'Well then, that being so, isn't body liable to be quickly
10 dissolved, whereas soul must be completely indissoluble, or
something close to it?'
c 'Of course.'

'Now you're aware that when a human being has died,
the part of him that's seen, his body, which is situated in
the seen world, the corpse as we call it, although liable to
5 be dissolved and fall apart and to disintegrate, undergoes
none of those things at once, but remains as it is for a fairly
long time—in fact for a very considerable time, even if
someone dies with his body in beautiful condition, and in
the flower of youth; why, the body that is shrunken and
embalmed, like those who've been embalmed in Egypt,
d remains almost entire for an immensely long time; and
even should the body decay, some parts of it, bones and
sinews and all such things, are still practically immortal;
isn't that so?'
'Yes.'

5 'Can it be, then, that the soul, the invisible part, which
goes to another place of that kind, noble, pure, and
invisible, to "Hades" in the true sense of the word,* into
the presence of the good and wise God—where, God
willing, my own soul too must shortly enter—can it be that
this, which we've found to be a thing of such a kind and
10 nature, should on separation from the body at once be
e blown apart and perish, as most people say? Far from it,
my dear Cebes and Simmias; rather, the truth is far more
like this: suppose it is separated in purity, while trailing
nothing of the body with it, since it had no avoidable
5 commerce with it during life, but shunned it; suppose too
that it has been gathered together alone into itself, since it
always cultivated this—nothing else but the right practice
81 of philosophy, in fact, the cultivation of dying without
complaint—wouldn't that be the cultivation of death?'
'It certainly would.'

'If it is in that state, then, does it not depart to the
5 invisible which is similar to it, the divine and immortal and
wise; and on arrival there, isn't its lot to be happy, released
from its wandering and folly, its fears and wild lusts, and

other ills of the human condition, and as is said of the
initiated, does it not pass the rest of time in very truth with   10
gods? Are we to say, that Cebes, or something else?'

'That, most certainly!' said Cebes.

'Whereas, I imagine, if it is separated from the body   b
when it has been polluted and made impure, because it has
always been with the body, has served and loved it, and
been so bewitched by it, by its passions and pleasures, that
it thinks nothing else real save what is corporeal—what can   5
be touched and seen, drunk and eaten, or used for sexual
enjoyment—yet it has been accustomed to hate and shun
and tremble before what is obscure to the eyes and
invisible, but intelligible and grasped by philosophy; do   c
you think a soul in that condition will separate unsullied,
and alone by itself?'

'By no means.'

'Rather, I imagine, it will have been interspersed with a
corporeal element, ingrained in it by the body's company   5
and intercourse, through constant association and much
training?'

'Certainly.'

'And one must suppose, my friend, that this element is
ponderous, that it is heavy and earthy and is seen; and thus
encumbered, such a soul is weighed down, and dragged   10
back into the region of the seen, through fear of the
invisible and of Hades; and it roams among tombs and   d
graves, so it is said, around which some shadowy phantoms
of souls have actually been seen, such wraiths as souls of
that kind afford, souls that have been released in no pure
condition, but while partaking in the seen; and that is just
why they are seen.'

'That's likely, Socrates.'   5

'It is indeed, Cebes; and they're likely to be the souls not
of the good but of the wicked, that are compelled to
wander about such places, paying the penalty for their
former nurture, evil as it was. And they wander about
until, owing to the desire of the corporeal element   e
attendant upon them, they are once more imprisoned in a
body; and they're likely to be imprisoned in whatever types

33

of character they may have cultivated in their lifetime.'*

'What types can you mean, Socrates?'

5 'Those who have cultivated gluttony, for example, and lechery, and drunkenness, and have taken no pains to 82 avoid them, are likely to enter the forms of donkeys and animals of that sort. Don't you think so?'

'What you say is very likely.'

'Yes, and those who've preferred injustice, tyranny, and robbery will enter the forms of wolves and hawks and 5 kites. Where else can we say that such souls will go?'

'Into such creatures, certainly,' said Cebes.

'And isn't the direction taken by the others as well obvious in each case, acording to the affinities of their training?'

'Quite obvious, of course.'

10 'And aren't the happiest among those and the ones who b enter the best place, those who have practised popular and social goodness, "temperance" and "justice" so-called, developed from habit and training, but devoid of philosophy and intelligence?'

'In what way are those happiest?'

5 'Because they're likely to go back into a race of tame and social creatures similar to their kind, bees perhaps, or wasps or ants; and to return to the human race again, and be born from those kinds as decent men.'

'That's likely.'

10 'But the company of gods may not rightly be joined by one who has not practised philosophy and departed in c absolute purity, by any but the lover of knowledge. It's for those reasons, Simmias and Cebes, my friends, that true philosophers abstain from all bodily desires, and stand firm without surrendering to them; it's not for any fear of 5 poverty or loss of estate, as with most people who are lovers of riches; nor again do they abstain through dread of dishonour or ill-repute attaching to wickedness, like lovers of power and prestige.'

'No, that would ill become them, Socrates,' said Cebes.

d 'Most certainly it would! And that, Cebes, is just why those who have any care for their own souls, and don't live fashioning the body, disregard all those people; they do not walk on the same paths as those who, in their view, don't know where they are going; but they themselves believe that their actions must not oppose philosophy, or the release and purifying rite it affords, and they are turned to follow it, in the direction in which it guides them.'

'How so, Socrates?'

'I'll tell you. Lovers of knowledge recognize that when philosophy takes their soul in hand, it has been veritably bound and glued to the body, and is forced to view things as if through a prison, rather than alone by itself; and that it is wallowing in utter ignorance. Now philosophy discerns the cunning of the prison, sees how it is effected through desire, so that the captive himself may co-operate most of all in his imprisonment. As I say, then, lovers of knowledge recognize that their soul is in that state when philosophy takes it in hand, gently reassures it and tries to release it, by showing that inquiry through the eyes is full of deceit, and deceitful too is inquiry through the ears and other senses; and by persuading it to withdraw from those, so far as it need not use them, and by urging it to collect and gather itself together, and to trust none other but itself, whenever, alone by itself, it thinks of any reality, alone by itself; and not to regard as real what it observes by other means, and what varies in various things; that kind of thing is sensible and seen, whereas the object of its own vision is intelligible and invisible. It is, then, just because it believes it should not oppose that release that the soul of the true philosopher abstains from pleasures and desires and pains, so far as it can, reckoning that when one feels intense pleasure or fear, pain, or desire, one incurs harm from them not merely to the extent that might be supposed—by being ill, for example, or spending money to satisfy one's desires—but one incurs the greatest and most extreme of all evils, and does not take it into account.'

'And what is that, Socrates?' said Cebes.

'It's that the soul of every human being, when intensely pleased or pained at something, is forced at the same time to suppose that whatever most affects it in this way is most clear and most real, when it is not so; and such objects especially are things seen, aren't they?'

'Certainly.'

d 'Well, isn't it in this experience that soul is most thoroughly bound fast by body?'

'How so?'

'Because each pleasure and pain fastens it to the body
5 with a sort of rivet, pins it there, and makes it corporeal, so that it takes for real whatever the body declares to be so. Since by sharing opinions and pleasures with the body, it is, I believe, forced to become of like character and nurture to
10 it, and to be incapable of entering Hades in purity; but it
e must always exit contaminated by the body, and so quickly fall back into another body, and grow in it as if sown there, and so have no part in communion with the divine and pure and uniform.'

'What you say is perfectly true, Socrates,' said Cebes.

5 'It's for those reasons, then, Cebes, that those who deserve to be called "lovers of knowledge" are orderly and brave; it's not for the reasons that count with most people; or do you think it is?'

84 'No, indeed I don't.'

'Indeed not; but the soul of a philosophic man would reason as we've said: it would not think that while philosophy should release it, yet on being released, it
5 should of itself surrender to pleasures and pains, to bind it to the body once again, and should perform the endless task of a Penelope working in reverse at a kind of web.* Rather, securing rest from those feelings, by following reasoning and being ever within it, and by beholding what
b is true and divine and not the object of opinion,* and being nurtured by it, it believes that it must live thus for as long as it lives, and that when it has died, it will enter that which
5 is akin and of like nature to itself, and be rid of human ills. With that kind of nurture, surely, Simmias and Cebes, there's no danger of its fearing that on separation from the body it may be rent apart, blown away by winds, go flying off, and exist no longer anywhere at all.'

When Socrates had said this, there was silence for a long   c
time. To judge from his appearance, Socrates himself was
absorbed in the foregoing argument, and so were most of
us; but Cebes and Simmias went on talking to each other in
a low voice. When he noticed them, Socrates asked: 'What   5
is it? Can it be that you find something lacking in what's
been said? It certainly still leaves room for many misgivings
and objections, if, that is, one's going to examine it
adequately. If it's something else you're considering, never
mind; but if you have some difficulty about those matters,
don't hesitate to speak for yourselves and explain it, if you   d
think what was said could be improved in any way; or
again, enlist me too, if you think you'll get out of your
difficulty any better with my help.'

Simmias replied: 'All right, Socrates, I'll tell you the
truth. For some time each of us has had difficulties, and has   5
been prompting and telling the other to question you, from
eagerness to hear, but hesitating to make trouble, in case
you should find it unwelcome in your present misfortune.'

When Socrates heard this, he chuckled and said: 'Dear
me, Simmias! I'd certainly find it hard to convince other
people that I don't regard my present lot as a misfortune,
when I can't convince even you two, but you're afraid that   e
I'm more ill-humoured now than in my earlier life; you
must, it seems, think I have a poorer power of prophecy   5
than the swans, who when they realize they must die, then   85
sing more fully and sweetly than they've ever sung before,
for joy that they are departing into the presence of the god
whose servants they are. Though indeed mankind, because
of their own fear of death, malign the swans, and say that
they sing their farewell song in distress, lamenting their   5
death; they don't reflect that no bird sings when it is
hungry or cold or suffering any other distress, not even the
nightingale herself, nor the swallow, nor the hoopoe, birds
that are reputed to sing lamentations from distress. But, as
I see it, neither they nor the swans sing in distress, but   b
rather, I believe, because, belonging as they do to Apollo,
they are prophetic birds with foreknowledge of the
blessings of Hades, and therefore sing and rejoice more

greatly on that day than ever before. Now I hold that I
myself am a fellow-servant of the swans, consecrated to the
same god, that I possess prophetic power from my master
no less than theirs, and that I'm departing this life with as
good a cheer as they do. No: so far as that goes, you should
say and ask whatever you wish, for as long as eleven
Athenian gentlemen* allow.'

'Thank you,' said Simmias; 'then I'll tell you my
difficulty, and Cebes here in his turn will say where he
doesn't accept what's been said. I think, Socrates, as
perhaps you do too, that in these matters certain knowledge
is either impossible or very hard to come by in this life; but
that even so, not to test what is said about them in every
possible way, without leaving off till one has examined
them exhaustively from every aspect, shows a very feeble
spirit; on these questions one must achieve one of two
things: either learn or find out how things are; or, if that's
impossible, then adopt the best and least refutable of
human doctrines, embarking on it as a kind of raft, and
risking the dangers of the voyage through life, unless one
could travel more safely and with less risk, on a securer
conveyance afforded by some divine doctrine. So now I
shan't scruple to put my question, since you tell me to, and
then I shan't reproach myself at a later time for failing to
speak my mind now. In my view, Socrates, when I examine
what's been said, either alone or with Cebes here, it doesn't
seem altogether adequate.'

'Maybe your view is correct, my friend,' said Socrates;
'but tell me, in what way inadequate?'

'I think in this way,' he said: 'one could surely use the
same argument about the attunement of a lyre and its
strings,* and say that the attunement is something unseen
and incorporeal and very lovely and divine in the tuned
lyre, while the lyre itself and its strings are corporeal bodies
and composite and earthy and akin to the mortal. Now, if
someone smashed the lyre, or severed and snapped its
strings, suppose it were maintained, by the same argument
as yours, that the attunement must still exist and not have
perished—because it would be inconceivable that when the

strings had been snapped, the lyre and the strings themselves, which are of mortal nature, should still exist, and yet that the attunement, which has affinity and kinship to the b divine and the immortal, should have perished—and perished before the mortal; rather, it might be said, the attunement itself must still exist somewhere, and the wood and the strings would have to rot away before anything 5 happened to it. And in point of fact, Socrates, my own belief is that you're aware yourself that something of this sort is what we actually take the soul to be:* our body is kept in tension, as it were, and held together by hot and cold, dry and wet, and the like, and our soul is a blending c and attunement of these same things, when they're blended with each other in due proportion. If, then, the soul proves to be some kind of attunement, it's clear that when our body is unduly relaxed or tautened by illnesses and other 5 troubles, then the soul must perish at once, no matter how divine it may be, just like other attunements, those in musical notes and in all the products of craftsmen; whereas the remains of each body will last for a long time, until they're burnt up or rot away. Well, consider what we shall d say in answer to that argument, if anyone should claim that the soul, being a blending of the bodily elements, is the first thing to perish in what is called death.'

At this Socrates looked at us wide-eyed, as he often used 5 to, and said with a smile: 'Simmias' remarks are certainly fair. So if any of you is more resourceful than I am, why doesn't he answer him? Because he really seems to be coming to grips with the argument in no mean fashion. However, before answering I think we should first hear e from Cebes here what further charge he has to bring against the argument, so that in the intervening period we may be thinking what to say; then, when we've heard them both, either we can agree with them, if it seems they're at all in tune; or if not, we can enter a plea for the argument at 5 that point. Come on then, Cebes, tell us what's been troubling you.'

'I certainly will,' said Cebes. 'You see, the argument seems to me to remain where it was, and to be open to the

87 same charge as we made before. As to the existence of our soul even before it entered its present form, I don't take back my admission that that has been very neatly, and, if it's not presumptuous to say so, very adequately proved; but I don't think the same about its still existing somewhere
5 when we've died. Not that I agree with Simmias' objection that soul isn't stronger and longer-lived than body: because I think it far superior in all those ways. "Why then", the argument would say, "are you still in doubt, when you can
b see that the weaker part still exists after the person has died? Don't you think the longer-lived part must still be preserved during that time?"

'Well, consider if there's anything in my reply to that; because it seems that, like Simmias, I too need an image. What's being said, I think, is very much as if someone
5 should offer this argument about a person—a weaver who has died in old age—to show that the person hasn't perished but exists somewhere intact, and should produce as evidence the fact that the cloak he had woven for himself, and worn, was intact and had not perished; and if
c anyone doubted him, he should ask which class of thing is longer-lived, a human being, or a cloak in constant use and wear; and on being answered that a human being is much longer-lived, should think it had been proved that the
5 person must therefore surely be intact, seeing that something shorter-lived hadn't perished. Yet in fact, Simmias, that isn't so: because you too must consider what I'm saying. Everyone would object that that is a simple-minded argument. Because this weaver, though he'd woven and
d worn out many such cloaks, perished after all of them, despite their number, but still, presumably, before the last one; and yet for all that a human being is neither lesser nor weaker than a cloak.

'The relation of soul to body would, I think, admit of the same comparison: anyone making the same points about them, that the soul is long-lived, while the body is weaker
5 and shorter-lived, would in my view argue reasonably; true indeed, he might say, every soul wears out many bodies, especially in a life of many years because, though the body

40

may decay and perish while the person is still alive, still the
soul will always weave afresh what's being worn out;   e
nevertheless, when the soul does perish, it will have to be
wearing its last garment, and must perish before that one
alone; and when the soul has perished, then at last the body
will reveal its natural weakness, moulder away quickly,   5
and be gone. So we've no right as yet to trust that
argument, and feel confident that our soul still exists   88
somewhere after we've died. Indeed, were one to grant the
speaker even more than what you say, allowing him not
only that our souls existed in the time before we were born,
but that nothing prevents the souls of some, even after
we've died, from still existing and continuing to exist, and   5
from being born and dying over and over again—because
soul is so strong by nature that it can endure repeated
births—even allowing all that, were one not to grant the
further point that it does not suffer in its many births, and
does not end by perishing completely in one of its deaths,   10
and were one to say that no one can know that death or   b
detachment from the body which brings perishing to the
soul—since none of us can possibly perceive it—well, if
that's the case, then anyone who's confident in face of
death must be possessed of a foolish confidence, unless he
can prove that soul is completely immortal and imperish-   5
able; otherwise, anyone about to die must always fear for
his own soul, lest in its present disjunction from the body it
perish completely.'

All of us who heard them were disagreeably affected by   c
their words, as we afterwards told one another: we'd been
completely convinced by the earlier argument, yet now
they seemed to disturb us again, and make us doubtful not
only about the arguments already put forward but also   5
about points yet to be raised, for fear that we were
incompetent judges of anything, or even that these things
might be inherently doubtful.

Echecrates. Goodness, Phaedo, you have my sympathy.
Because now that I've heard you, it occurs to me to say to   d
myself something like this: 'What argument shall we ever

41

trust now? How thoroughly convincing was the argument
that Socrates gave, yet now it's fallen into discredit.' That
5 theory that our soul is a kind of attunement has a strange
hold on me, now as it always has done, so your statement
of it has served to remind me that I'd formerly held that
view myself. And I very much need some other argument
that will convince me once again, as if from the start, that
the soul of one who has died doesn't die with him. So do
e please tell me how Socrates pursued the discussion. Did he
become visibly troubled at all, as you say you were, or did
he come quietly to the argument's help? And was his help
adequate or deficient? Please relate everything to us, as
minutely as you can.

Phaedo. Well, Echecrates, often as I've admired
5 Socrates, I never found him more wonderful than when
89 with him then. That he should have had an answer to give
isn't, perhaps, surprising; but what I specially admired
was, first, the pleasure, kindliness, and approval with
which he received the young men's argument; next his
acuteness in perceiving how their speeches had affected us;
5 and finally his success in treating us, rallying us as if we
were fleeing in defeat, and encouraging us to follow him in
examining the argument together.

Echecrates. In what way?

Phaedo. I'll tell you. I happened to be sitting to his
b right, on a stool beside the bed, while he was a good way
above me. Stroking my head and gathering the hair on my
neck—it was his way now and again to make fun of my
5 hair—* he said: 'So tomorrow perhaps, Phaedo, you'll cut
off those lovely locks.'

'I expect so, Socrates,' I replied.

'You won't, if you listen to me.'

'What then?' I asked.

'Today', he said, 'I'll cut mine and you yours—if, that is,
10 the argument dies on us and we can't revive it. For myself,
c if I were you and the argument got away from me, I should
swear an oath, like the Argives,* not to grow my hair again
till I'd fought back and defeated the argument of Simmias
and Cebes.'

'But', I said, 'even Heracles is said to have been no match   5
for two.'

'Then summon me as your Iolaus,'* he said, 'while
there's still light.'

'All right,' I said, 'I summon you, not as if I were
Heracles myself, but rather as Iolaus summoning Heracles.'   10

'That will make no difference,' he said. 'But first let's
take care that a certain fate doesn't befall us.'

'What's that?' I asked.

'The fate of becoming "misologists",* just as some   d
become misanthropists; because there's no greater evil
that could befall anyone than this—the hating of
arguments. "Misology" and misanthropy both arise from   5
the same source. Misanthropy develops when, without
skill, one puts complete trust in somebody, thinking the
person absolutely true and sound and reliable, and then a
little later finds him bad and unreliable; and then that
happens again with another person; and when it happens
often, especially at the hands of those one would regard as   e
one's nearest and dearest friends, one ends up, after
repeated hard knocks, hating everyone, thinking there's no
soundness whatever in anyone at all. Have you never
noticed that happening?'

'I certainly have,' I said.

'Well, isn't it an ugly thing, and isn't it clear that such a   5
person was setting about handling human beings, without
any skill in human relations? Because if one handled them
with skill, one would surely have recognized the truth, that   90
extremely good and bad people are both very few in
number, and the majority lie in between.'

'What do you mean?' I asked.

'It's the same as with extremely small and large things:
do you think anything is rarer than finding an extremely   5
large or extremely small person, or dog, or anything else?
Or again, one that's extremely fast or slow, ugly or
beautiful, pale or dark? Haven't you noticed that in all
such cases extreme instances at either end are rare and few
in number, whereas intermediate ones are plentiful and
common?'

10 'Certainly,' I said.

b 'Don't you think, then, that if a contest in badness were promoted, there too those in the first class would be very few?'

'Probably,' I said.

'Yes, probably; though in that respect arguments aren't
5 like human beings, but I was following the lead you gave just now. The resemblance is found, rather, when someone who lacks skill in arguments, trusts some argument to be true, and then a little later it seems to him false, sometimes when it is, and sometimes when it isn't, and then the same thing happens with one argument after another—it is, as
c you know, especially those who've spent all their time on contradictory arguments,* who end up thinking they've become extremely wise: they alone have discerned that there's nothing sound or secure whatever, either in things or arguments; but that all realities are carried up and
5 down, just like things fluctuating in the Euripus,* and never remain at rest for any time.'

'What you say is perfectly true,' I said.

'Then, Phaedo, it would be a pitful fate, if there were in
d fact some true and secure argument, and one that could be discerned, yet owing to association with arguments of the sort that seem now true and now false, one blamed neither oneself nor one's own lack of skill, but finally relieved
5 one's distress by shifting the blame from oneself to arguments, and then finished out the rest of one's life hating and abusing arguments, and was deprived both of the truth and of knowledge of realities.'

'Goodness, that certainly would be pitiful,' I said.

'Then let's guard against that first, and let's not admit
e into our soul the thought that there's probably nothing sound in arguments; but let's far rather admit that we're not yet sound ourselves, but must strive manfully to
91 become sound—you and the others for the sake of your whole future life, but I because of death itself; since that very issue is one that I may not be facing as a philosopher should, but rather as one bent on victory, like those quite devoid of education. They too, when they dispute about

44

something, care nothing for the truth of the matter under
discussion, but are eager only that those present shall   5
accept their own thesis. It seems to me that on this occasion
I shall differ from them only to this extent: my concern will
not be, except perhaps incidentally, that what I say shall
seem true to those present, but rather that it shall, as far as
possible, seem so to myself. Because I reckon, my dear   b
friend—watch how anxious I am to score—that if what I
say proves true, it's surely well to have been persuaded;
whereas if there's nothing for a dead person, still, at least
during this very time before my death, I'll distress those   5
present less with lamentation, and this ignorance of mine
will not persist—that would be a bad thing—but will in a
little while be ended.

'Thus prepared, Simmias and Cebes, I advance against
the argument; but for your part, if you take my advice,
you'll care little for Socrates but much more for the truth: if   c
I seem to you to say anything true, agree with it; but if not,
resist it with every argument you can, taking care that in
my zeal I don't deceive you and myself alike, and go off like   5
a bee leaving its sting behind.

'Well now, to proceed. First remind me of what you were
saying, in case I prove not to have remembered. Simmias, I
believe, is doubtful and afraid that the soul, though more
divine and lovelier than the body, may still perish before it,   d
being a kind of attunement. Whereas Cebes, I thought,
agreed with me in this much, that soul is longer-lived than
body; but he held that no one could be sure whether the   5
soul, after wearing out many bodies time and again, might
not then perish itself, leaving its last body behind, and
whether death might not be just that, the perishing of
soul—since body, of course, is perishing incessantly and
never stops. Aren't those the points, Simmias and Cebes,
that we have to consider?'

They both agreed that they were.   e

'Then do you reject all of the previous arguments, or
only some of them?'

'Some of them,' they said, 'but not others.'

'Well what do you say, then, about the argument in   5

45

which we said that learning was recollection, and that that
92 being so, our souls must exist somewhere else before being
imprisoned in the body?'

'For my part,' said Cebes, 'I was wonderfully convinced
by it at the time, and remain so now, as by no other
argument.'

'And I'm of the same mind,' said Simmias; 'and I'd be
5 very surprised if I ever came to think otherwise about that.'

To this Socrates answered: 'But you'll have to think
otherwise, my Theban friend, if you stick to this idea that
attunement is a composite thing, and that soul is a kind of
attunement composed of the bodily elements held in
b tension; because you surely won't allow yourself to say
that an attunement existed as a composite, before the
elements of which it was to be composed; or will you?'

'Certainly not, Socrates.'

'Then do you see that that is implied by your assertion,
5 when you say that the soul exists before entering human
form and body, yet that it is a composite of things that
don't yet exist? Surely your attunement isn't, in fact, the
same kind of thing as that to which you liken it: rather, the
c lyre, and its strings and notes, come into being first, as yet
untuned, whereas the attunement is put together last of all,
and is the first to perish. So how's this theory of yours
going to harmonize with that one?'

'In no way,' said Simmias.

5 'Yet surely, if there's one theory that ought to be in
harmony, it's a theory about attunement.'

'So it ought,' said Simmias.

'Well, this one of yours isn't in harmony; but see which
of the theories you prefer: that learning is recollection, or
10 that soul is attunement.'

'The former, by a long way, Socrates. Because I acquired
d the latter without any proof, but from a certain likelihood
and plausibility about it, whence its appeal for most
people; but I'm aware that arguments basing their proofs
upon likelihoods are impostors, and if one doesn't guard
5 against them, they completely deceive one, in geometry as
well as in all other subjects. But the argument about

recollection and learning has come from a hypothesis worthy of acceptance. Because it was, of course, asserted that our soul existed even before it entered the body, just as surely as its object exists—the reality which bears the name of "that which it is";* and that, I'm convinced, I have e accepted rightly and for adequate reason. So it would seem, consequently, that I must allow neither myself nor anyone else to say that soul is attunement.'

'Again now, look at it this way, Simmias. Do you think it befits an attunement, or any other compound, to be in any 93 state other than that of the elements of which it's composed?'

'Certainly not.'

'Nor yet, I presume, to act, or be acted upon, in any way differently from the way they may act or be acted 5 upon?'

He assented.

'An attunement therefore should not properly direct the things of which it's composed, but should follow them.'

He agreed.

'Then an attunement can't possibly undergo contrary movement or utter sound or be opposed in any other way to its own parts.' 10

'It can't possibly.'

'Again now, isn't it natural for every attunement to be an attunement just as it's been tuned?'

'I don't understand.'

'Isn't it the case that if it's been tuned more and to a greater extent, assuming that to be possible, it will be more b an attunement* and a greater one; whereas if less and to a smaller extent, it will be a lesser and smaller one?'

'Certainly.'

'Well, is this the case with soul—that even in the least degree, one soul is either to a greater extent and more than 5 another, or to a smaller extent and less, just itself—namely, a soul?'

'In no way whatever.'

'Well, but is one soul said to have intelligence and goodness and to be good, while another is said to have folly c and wickedness and to be bad? And are we right in saying those things?'

'Quite right.'

'Then what will any of those who maintain that soul is attunement say these things are, existing in our souls—
5 goodness and badness? Are they, in turn, a further attunement and non-attunement?* And is one soul, the good one, tuned, and does it have within itself, being an attunement, a further attunement, whereas the untuned one is just itself, and lacking a further attunement within it?'

'I couldn't say myself,' said Simmias; 'but obviously
10 anyone maintaining the hypothesis would say something of that sort.'

d 'But it's already been agreed that no one soul is more or less a soul than another; and this is the admission that no one attunement is either more or to a greater extent, or less or to a smaller extent, an attunement than another.* Isn't that so?'

5 'Certainly.'

'But that which is neither more nor less an attunement has been neither more nor less tuned; is that so?'

'It is.'

'But does that which has been neither more nor less
10 tuned participate in attunement to a greater or to a smaller degree, or to an equal degree?'

'To an equal degree.'

'But then, given that no one soul is either more or less
e itself, namely a soul, than another, it hasn't been more or less tuned either?'

'That is so.'

'And that being its condition, surely it couldn't participate
5 more either in non-attunement or in attunement?'

'Indeed not.'

'And that again being its condition, could any one soul participate to a greater extent than another in badness or goodness, assuming that badness is non-attunement, while goodness is attunement?'

10 'It couldn't.'

'Or rather, surely, following sound reasoning, Simmias, **94** no soul will participate in badness, assuming it is attune- ment; because naturally an attunement, being completely itself, namely an attunement, could never participate in non-attunement.'

'No indeed.'   5

'Nor then, of course, could a soul, being completely a soul, participate in badness.'

'How could it, in view of what's already been said?'

'By that argument, then, we find that all souls of all living things will be equally good, assuming that it's the nature of souls to be equally themselves, namely souls.'   10

'So it seems to me, Socrates.'

'Yes, and do you approve of that assertion, or think that would happen to the argument, if the hypothesis that soul **b** is attunement were correct?'

'Not in the least.'

'Again now, would you say that of all the things in a person it is anything but soul, especially if it's a wise one, 5 that rules him?'

'Does it comply with the bodily feelings or does it oppose them? I mean, for example, when heat and thirst are in the body, by pulling the opposite way, away from drinking, and away from eating when it feels hunger; and surely in 10 countless other ways we see the soul opposing bodily   **c** feelings, don't we?'

'We certainly do.'

'And again, didn't we agree earlier that if it is attunement, it would never utter notes opposed to the tensions,   5 relaxations, strikings, and any other affections of its components, but would follow and never dominate them?'

'We did of course agree.'

'Well now, don't we find it, in fact, operating in just the opposite way, dominating all those alleged sources of its   10 existence, and opposing them in almost everything through- **d** out all of life, mastering them in all kinds of ways, sometimes disciplining more harshly and painfully with gymnastics and medicine, sometimes more mildly, now threatening and now admonishing, conversing with our

5 appetites and passions and fears, as if with a separate
thing? That, surely, is the sort of thing Homer has
represented in the *Odyssey*, where he says that Odysseus:

> Striking his breast, reproved his heart with the words:
e > "Endure, my heart; e'en worse thou didst once endure."*

Do you think he'd have composed that, with the idea that
the soul was attunement, the sort of thing that could be led
by the feelings of the body rather than something that
5 could lead and master them, being itself far too divine a
thing to rank as attunement?'

'Goodness no, Socrates, I don't!'

'In no way at all then, my friend, do we approve of the
95 thesis that soul is a kind of attunement; because it seems
that we should agree neither with the divine poet Homer
nor with ourselves.'

'That is so.'

'Well then,' said Socrates, 'we seem to have placated the
5 Theban lady Harmonia* moderately well; but now, how
about the question of Cadmus? How and with what
argument, Cebes, shall we placate him?'

'You'll find a way, I think,' said Cebes; 'at any rate this
argument of yours against attunement has surprised me
beyond expectation. Because when Simmias was speaking
b in his perplexity, I was very much wondering if anyone
would be able to handle his argument; so it seemed to me
quite remarkable that it immediately failed to withstand
the first assault of your own argument. Accordingly, I
shouldn't wonder if the argument of Cadmus suffered the
same fate.'

5 'No big talking, my friend,' said Socrates, 'in case some
evil eye* should turn the coming argument to rout. But that
shall be God's concern; for ourselves, let's come to close
quarters, in Homeric fashion, and try to see if, in fact,
there's anything in what you say. The sum and substance of
c what you're after is surely this: you want it proved that our
soul is imperishable and immortal, if a philosophic man
about to die, confidently believing that after death he'll fare

much better yonder than if he were ending a life lived differently, isn't to be possessed of a senseless and foolish confidence. As for showing that the soul is something 5 strong and god-like, and existed even before we were born as human beings, nothing prevents all that, you say, from indicating not immortality, but only that soul is long-lived and existed somewhere for an immense length of time in the past, and knew and did all kinds of things; even so, it was none the more immortal for all that, but its very entry d into a human body was the beginning of its perishing, like an illness: it lives this life in distress, and finally perishes in what is called death. And, you say, it makes no difference, so far as our individual fears are concerned, whether it 5 enters a body once or many times: anyone who neither knows nor can give proof that it's immortal should be afraid, unless he has no sense.

'Something like that, Cebes, is what I think you're e saying; and I'm purposely reviewing it more than once, so that nothing may escape us, and so that you may add or take away anything you wish.'

To this Cebes replied: 'No, there's nothing at present 5 that I want to take away or add; those are my very points.'

Here Socrates paused for a long time examining something in his own mind. He then said: 'It's no trivial matter, this quest of yours, Cebes: it calls for a thorough inquiry into the whole question of the reason* for coming-to-be 96 and destruction.* So I will, if you like, relate my own experiences on these matters: and then, if any of the things I say seem helpful to you, you can use them for conviction on the points you raise.'

'Well, I certainly should like that,' said Cebes. 5

'Then listen to my story. When I was young, Cebes, I was remarkably keen on the kind of wisdom known as natural science; it seemed to me splendid to know the reasons for each thing, why each thing comes to be, why it perishes, 10 and why it exists. And I was always shifting back and b forth, examining, for a start, questions like these:* is it, as some said, whenever the hot and the cold give rise to putrefaction, that living creatures develop? And is it blood

51

5 that we think with, or air, or fire? Or is it none of those, but the brain that provides the senses of hearing and seeing and smelling, from which memory and judgement come to be; and is it from memory and judgement, when they've acquired stability, that knowledge comes to be accordingly?

c Next, when I went on to examine the destruction of those things, and what happens in the heavens and the earth, I finally judged myself to have absolutely no gift for that kind of inquiry. I'll tell you a good enough sign of this: there had been things that I previously did know for sure, at least as I
5 myself and others thought; yet I was then so utterly blinded by this inquiry, that I unlearned even those things I formerly supposed I knew,* including, amongst many other things, why it is that a human being grows. That, I
d used earlier to suppose, was obvious to everyone: it was because of eating and drinking; whenever, from food, flesh came to accrue to flesh, and bone to bone, and similarly on the same principle the appropriate matter came to accrue to each of the other parts, it was then that the little bulk
5 later came to be big; and in this way the small human being comes to be large. That was what I supposed then: reasonably enough, don't you think?'

'I do,' said Cebes.

'Well, consider these further cases: I used to suppose it was an adequate view, whenever a large person standing
e beside a small one appeared to be larger just by a head;* similarly with two horses. And, to take cases even clearer than these, it seemed to me that ten was greater than eight because of the accruing of two to the latter, and that two cubits were larger than one cubit, because of their exceeding the latter by half.'*

5 'Well, what do you think about them now?' said Cebes.

'I can assure you that I'm far from supposing I know the reason for any of those things, when I don't even accept from myself that when you add one to one, it's either the one to which the addition is made that's come to be two, or
97 the one that's been added and the one to which it's been added, that have come to be two, because of the addition of one to the other. Because I wonder if, when they were apart

from each other, each was one and they weren't two then; whereas when they came close to each other, this then became a reason for their coming to be two—the union in 5 which they were juxtaposed.* Nor again can I any longer be persuaded, if you divide one, that this has now become a reason for its coming to be two, namely division; because if so, we have a reason opposite to the previous one* for its b coming to be two; then it was their being brought close to each other and added, one to the other; whereas now it's their being drawn apart, and separated each from the other. Why, I can't even persuade myself any longer that I know why it is that one comes to be; nor, in short, why 5 anything else comes to be, or perishes, or exists, following that method of inquiry. Instead I rashly adopt a different method, a jumble of my own, and in no way incline towards the other.

'One day, however, I heard someone reading from a book he said was by Anaxagoras,* according to which it is, in fact, intelligence that orders and is the reason for c everything. Now this was a reason that pleased me; it seemed to me, somehow, to be a good thing that intelligence should be the reason for everything. And I thought that, if that's the case, then intelligence in ordering 5 all things must order them and place each individual thing in the best way possible; so if anyone wanted to find out the reason why each thing comes to be or perishes or exists, this is what he must find out about it: how is it best for that d thing to exist, or to act or be acted upon in any way? On this theory, then, a person should consider nothing else, whether in regard to himself or anything else, but the best, the highest good; though the same person must also know the worse, as they are objects of the same knowledge. 5 Reckoning thus, I was pleased to think I'd found, in Anaxagoras, an instructor in the reason for things to suit my own intelligence. And I thought he'd inform me, first, whether the earth is flat or round, and when he'd informed e me, he'd go on to expound the reason why it must be so, telling me what was better—better, that is, that it should be like this; and if he said it was in the centre, he'd go on to

expound the view that a central position for it was better. If
98 he could make those things clear to me, I was prepared to
hanker no more after any other kind of reason. What's
more, I was prepared to find out in just the same way about
the sun, the moon, and the stars, about their relative
velocity and turnings and the other things that happen to
5 them, and how it's better for each of them to act and be
acted upon just as they are. Because I never supposed that,
having said they were ordered by intelligence, he'd bring in
any reason for them other than its being best for them to be
b just the way they are; and I supposed that in assigning the
reason for each individual thing, and for things in general,
he'd go on to expound what was best for the individual,
and what was the common good for all; nor would I have
sold those hopes for a large sum, but I made all haste to get
5 hold of the books and read them as quickly as I could, so
that I might know as quickly as possible what was best and
what was worse.

'Well, my friend, those marvellous hopes of mine were
dashed; because, as I went on with my reading, I beheld a
man making no use of his intelligence at all,* nor finding in
c it any reasons for the ordering of things, but imputing them
to such things as air and ether and water and many other
absurdities. In fact, he seemed to me to be in exactly the
position of someone who said that all Socrates' actions
5 were performed with his intelligence, and who then tried to
give the reasons for each of my actions by saying, first, that
the reason why I'm now sitting here is that my body
consists of bones and sinews, and the bones are hard and
separated from each other by joints, whereas the sinews,
d which can be tightened and relaxed, surround the bones,
together with the flesh and the skin that holds them
together; so that when the bones are turned in their
sockets, the sinews by stretching and tensing enable me
somehow to bend my limbs at this moment, and that's the
5 reason why I'm sitting here bent in this way; or again, by
mentioning other reasons of the same kind for my talking
with you, imputing it to vocal sounds, air currents,
auditory sensations, and countless other such things, yet

neglecting to mention the true reasons: that Athenians   98e
judged it better to condemn me, and therefore I in my turn
have judged it better to sit here, and thought it more just to
stay behind and submit to such penalty as they may ordain.   5
Because, I dare swear,* these sinews and bones would long   99
since have been off in Megara or Boeotia, impelled by their
judgement of what was best, had I not thought it more just
and honourable not to escape and run away, but to submit
to whatever penalty the city might impose. But to call such   5
things "reasons" is quite absurd. It would be quite true to
say that without possessing such things as bones and
sinews, and whatever else I possess, I shouldn't be able to
do what I judged best; but to call those things the reasons
for my actions, rather than my choice of what is best, and   b
that too though I act with intelligence, would be a
thoroughly loose way of talking. Fancy being unable to
distinguish two different things: the reason proper, and
that without which the reason could never be a reason! Yet
it's this latter that most people call a reason, appearing to   5
me to be feeling it over blindfold,* as it were, and applying
a wrong name to it. That's why one man makes the earth
stay in position by means of the heaven, putting a whirl
around it; while another presses down the air as a base, as
if with a flat kneading-trough.* Yet the power by which
they're now situated in the best way that they could be   c
placed, this they neither look for nor credit with any
supernatural strength; but they think they'll one day
discover an Atlas stronger and more immortal than that,*
who does more to hold everything together. That it's the
good or binding,* that genuinely does bind and hold things   5
together, they don't believe at all. Now I should most
gladly have become anyone's pupil, to learn the truth about
a reason of that sort; but since I was deprived of that,
proving unable either to find it for myself or to learn it
from anyone else, would you like me, Cebes, to give you a   d
display of how I've conducted my second voyage in quest
of the reason?'*

   'Yes, I'd like that immensely,' he said.
   'Well then, it seemed to me next, since I'd been wearing

5 myself out studying things, that I must take care not to incur what happens to people who observe and examine the sun during an eclipse; some of them, you know, ruin

e their eyes, unless they examine its image in water or something of that sort. I had a similar thought: I was afraid I might be completely blinded in my soul, by looking at objects with my eyes and trying to lay hold of them with

5 each of my senses. So I thought I should take refuge in theories,* and study the truth of matters in them. Perhaps

100 my comparison is, in a certain way, inept; as I don't at all admit that one who examines things in theories is any more studying them in images than one who examines them in concrete.* But anyhow, this was how I proceeded: positing

5 on each occasion the theory I judge strongest, I put down as true whatever things seem to me to accord with it, both about a reason and about everything else; and whatever do not, I put down as not true. But I'd like to explain my meaning more clearly; because I don't imagine you understand it as yet.'

'Not entirely, I must say!' said Cebes.

b 'Well, this is what I mean: it's nothing new, but what I've spoken of incessantly in our earlier discussion as well as at other times. I'm going to set about displaying to you the

5 kind of reason I've been dealing with; and I'll go back to those much harped-on entities,* and start from them, positing the existence of a beautiful, itself by itself, and of a good and a large and all the rest. If you grant me that and agree that those things exist, I hope that from them I shall display to you the reason, and find out that soul is immortal.'

c 'Well, you may certainly take that for granted,' said Cebes, 'so you couldn't be too quick to conclude.'

'Then consider the next point, and see if you think as I do. It seems to me that if anything else is beautiful besides

5 the beautiful itself, it is beautiful for no reason at all other than that it participates in that beautiful; and the same goes for all of them. Do you assent to a reason of that kind?'

'I do.'

'Then I no longer understand nor can I recognize those other clever reasons; but if anyone gives me as the reason why a given thing is beautiful either its having a blooming colour, or its shape, or something else like that, I dismiss those other things—because all those others confuse me—but in a plain, artless, and possibly simple-minded way, I hold this close to myself: nothing else makes it beautiful except that beautiful itself, whether by its presence or communion or whatever the manner and nature of the relation may be;* as I don't go so far as to affirm that, but only that it is by the beautiful that all beautiful things are beautiful. Because that seems to be the safest answer to give both to myself and to another, and if I hang on to that, I believe I'll never fall: it's safe to answer both to myself and to anyone else that it is by the beautiful* that beautiful things are beautiful; or don't you agree?'

'I do.'

'Similarly it's by largeness that large things are large, and larger things larger, and by smallness that smaller things are smaller?'

'Yes.'

'Then you too wouldn't accept anyone's saying that one person was larger than another by a head, and that the smaller was smaller by the same thing; but you'd protest that you for your part will say only that everything larger than something else is larger by nothing but largeness, and largeness is the reason for its being larger; and that the smaller is smaller by nothing but smallness, and smallness is the reason for its being smaller. You'd be afraid, I imagine, of meeting the following contradiction: if you say that someone is larger and smaller by a head, then, first, the larger will be larger and the smaller smaller by the same thing;* and secondly, the head, by which the larger person is larger, is itself a small thing; and it's surely monstrous that anyone should be large by something small;* or wouldn't you be afraid of that?'

'Yes, I should,' said Cebes laughing.

'Then wouldn't you be afraid to say that ten is greater than eight by two, and that that is the reason for its

57

exceeding, rather than that it's by numerousness, and because of numerousness? Or that two cubits are larger than one cubit by half, rather than by largeness? Because, of course, there'd be the same fear.'

'Certainly,' he said.

'And again, wouldn't you beware of saying that when one is added to one, the addition is the reason for their
c coming to be two, or when one is divided, that division is the reason? You'd shout loudly that you know no other way in which each thing comes to be, except by participating in the particular reality of any given thing in which it
5 does participate; and in those cases you own no other reason for their coming to be two, save participation in twoness:* things that are going to be two must participate in that, and whatever is going to be one must participate in oneness. You'd dismiss those divisions and additions and other such subtleties, leaving them as answers to be given
d by people wiser than yourself; but you, scared of your own shadow, as the saying is,* and of your inexperience, would cling to the safety of the hypothesis, and answer accordingly. But if anyone fastened upon the hypothesis itself,* you would dismiss him, and you wouldn't answer till you should have examined its consequences, to see if, in your
5 view, they are in accord or discord with each other; and when you had to give an account of the hypothesis itself, you would give it in the same way, once again positing
e another hypothesis, whichever should seem best of those above, till you came to something adequate;* but you wouldn't jumble things as the contradiction-mongers do,* by discussing the starting-point and its consequences at the same time, if, that is, you wanted to discover any realities. For them, perhaps, that isn't a matter of the least thought
5 or concern; their wisdom enables them to mix everything up together, yet still be pleased with themselves; but you, if
102 you really are a philosopher, would, I imagine, do as I say.'

'What you say is perfectly true,' said Simmias and Cebes together.

Echecrates. Goodness, Phaedo, there was reason to say

that! It seems marvellous to me how clearly he put things, even for someone of small intelligence.   5

Phaedo.   Exactly, Echecrates. That was how it seemed to everyone there.

Echecrates.   And to us who weren't there but are now hearing it. But how did the discussion continue?

Phaedo.   As I recall, when those points had been   10
granted him, and it was agreed that each of the forms   b
existed, and that the other things, partaking in them, took
the name of the forms themselves, he next asked: 'If you
say that that is so, then whenever you say that Simmias is
larger than Socrates but smaller than Phaedo, you mean   5
then, don't you, that both things are in Simmias, largeness
and smallness?'*

'I do.'

'But now, do you agree that Simmias' overtopping of
Socrates isn't expressed in those words according to the
truth of the matter? Because it isn't, surely, by nature that   c
Simmias overtops him, by virtue, that is, of his being
Simmias,* but by virtue of the largeness that he happens to
have. Nor again does he overtop Socrates because Socrates
is Socrates, but because of smallness that Socrates has in
relation to his largeness?'   5

'True.'

'Nor again is he overtopped by Phaedo in virtue of
Phaedo's being Phaedo, but because of largeness that
Phaedo has in relation to Simmias' smallness?'

'That is so.'

'So that's how Simmias takes the name of being both   10
small and large; it's because he's between the two of them,
submitting his smallness to the largeness of the one for it to   d
overtop, and presenting to the other his largeness which
overtops the latter's smallness.'

At this he smiled, and added: 'That sounds as if I'm
going to talk like a book.* But anyway, things are surely as
I say.'

He agreed.

'I say this for the following reason, wanting you to think   5 as I do. It seems to me that not only is largeness itself never willing to be large and small at the same time, but also that the largeness in us never admits the small,* nor is it willing to be overtopped. Rather, one of two things must happen:

e either it must retreat and get out of the way, when its opposite, the small, advances towards it; or else, upon that opposite's advance, it must perish.* But what it is not willing to do is to abide and admit smallness, and thus be other than what it was. Thus I, having admitted and abided

5 smallness, am still what I am, this same individual, only small; whereas the large in us, while being large, can't endure to be small. And similarly, the small that's in us is not willing ever to come to be, or to be, large. Nor will any

103 other of the opposites, while still being what it was, at the same time come to be, and be, its own opposite. If that befalls it, either it goes away or it perishes.'

'I entirely agree,' said Cebes.

On hearing this, one of those present—I don't remember

5 for sure who it was—said: 'But look here, wasn't the very opposite of what's now being said agreed in our earlier discussion:* that the larger comes to be from the smaller, and the smaller from the larger, and that coming-to-be is, for opposites, just this—they come to be from their opposites. Whereas now I think it's being said that that

10 could never happen.'

Socrates turned his head and listened. 'It's splendid of

b you to have recalled that,' he said; 'but you don't realize the difference between what's being said now and what was said then. It was said then that one opposite thing comes to be from another opposite thing, what we're

5 saying now is that the opposite itself could never come to be opposite to itself, whether it be the opposite in us or the opposite in nature. Then, my friend, we were talking about things that have opposites, calling them by the names they take from them; whereas now we're talking about the opposites themselves, from whose presence in them the

c things so called derive their names. It's these latter that we're saying would never be willing to admit coming-to-be from each other.'

With this he looked towards Cebes and said: 'Cebes, you weren't troubled, I suppose, by any of the things our friend here said, were you?'

'No, not this time,' said Cebes; 'though I don't deny that many things do trouble me.'

'We've agreed, then, unreservedly on this point: an opposite will never be opposite to itself.'

'Completely.'

'Now please consider this further point, and see if you agree with it. Is there something you call hot, and again cold?'

'There is.'

'Do you mean the same as snow and fire?'

'No, most certainly not.'

'Rather, the hot is something different from fire, and the cold is something different from snow?'*

'Yes.'

'But this I think you will agree: what is snow will never, on the lines of what we were saying earlier, admit the hot and still be what it was, namely snow, and also hot; but at the advance of the hot, it will either get out of the way or perish.'

'Certainly.'

'And again fire, when cold advances, will either get out of the way or perish; but it will never endure to admit the coldness, and still be what it was, namely fire and also cold.'

'That's true.'

'The situation, then, in some cases of that kind, is as follows: not only is the form itself entitled to its own name for all time; but there's something else too, which is not the same as the form, but which, whenever it exists, always has the character of that form. Perhaps what I mean will be clearer in this further example: the odd must, surely, always be given this name that we're now using, mustn't it?'

'Certainly,'

'But is it the only thing there is—this is my question—or is there something else, which is not the same as the odd, **104**

yet which one must also always call odd, as well as by its
own name, because it is by nature such that it can never be
separated from the odd? I mean the sort of thing that
5 happens to threeness, and to many other instances.
Consider the case of threeness.* Don't you think it must
always be called both by its own name and by that of the
odd, although the odd is not the same as threeness? They
aren't the same, yet threeness and fiveness and half the
b entire number series are by nature, each of them, always
odd, although they are not the same as the odd. And again,
two and four and the whole of the other row of numbers,
though not the same as the even, are still, each of them,
always even. Do you agree or not?'

5 'Of course.'

'Look closely then at what I want to show. It is this:
apparently it's not only the opposites we spoke of that
don't admit each other. This is also true of all things which,
although not opposites to each other, always have the
10 opposites. These things too, it seems, don't admit whatever
c form may be opposite to the one that's in them, but when it
attacks, either they perish or they get out of the way. Thus
we shall say, shan't we, that three will sooner perish, will
undergo anything else whatever, sooner than abide coming
to be even, while remaining three?'

'Indeed we shall,' said Cebes.

5 'Moreover, twoness isn't opposite to threeness.'

'Indeed not.'

'Then not only do the forms that are opposites not abide
each other's attack; but there are, in addition, certain other
things that don't abide the opposites' attack.'*

10 'Quite true.'

'Then would you like us, if we can, to define what kinds
those are?'

'Certainly.'

d 'Would they, Cebes, be these: things that are compelled
by whatever occupies them to have not only its own form,
but always the form of some opposite as well?'*

'What do you mean?'

5 'As we were saying just now. You recognize, no doubt,

that whatever the form of three occupies must be not only three but also odd.'

'Certainly.'

'Then, we're saying, the form opposite to the character that has that effect could never go to a thing of that kind.'   10

'It couldn't.'

'But it was that of odd that had that effect?'

'Yes.'

'And opposite to that is that of the even?'

'Yes.'   15

'So that of the even will never come to three.'   e

'No, it won't.'

'Three, then, has no part in the even.'

'No part.'   5

'So threeness is uneven.'

'Yes.'

'So what I was saying we were to define, the kind of things which, while not opposite to a given thing, nevertheless don't admit it, the opposite in question—as we've just seen that threeness, while not opposite to the even, nevertheless doesn't admit it, since it always brings up its   10 opposite, just as twoness brings up the opposite of the odd, and the fire brings up the opposite of the cold, and so on in a great many other cases—well, see whether you would   105 define them thus: it is not only the opposite that doesn't admit its opposite; there is also that which brings up an opposite into whatever it enters itself; and that thing, the very thing that brings it up, never admits the quality   5 opposed to the one that's brought up. Recall it once more: there's no harm in hearing it several times. Five won't admit the form of the even, nor will ten, its double, admit that of the odd.* That, of course, is itself also the opposite of something else; nevertheless, it won't admit the form of   b the odd. Nor again will one-and-a-half, and the rest of that series, the halves, admit the form of the whole; and the same applies to a third, and all that series.* Do you follow and agree that that is so?'

'I agree most emphatically, and I do follow.'

'Then please repeat it from the start; and don't answer in   5 the exact terms of my question, but in imitation of my example. I say this, because from what's now being said I see a different kind of safety beyond the answer I gave initially, the old safe one. Thus, if you were to ask me what

c it is, by whose presence in a body, that body will be hot, I shan't give you the old safe, ignorant answer,* that it's heat, but a subtler answer now available, that it's fire. And again, if you ask what it is, by whose presence in a body, that body will ail, I shan't say that it's illness, but fever.

5 And again, if asked what it is, by whose presence in a number, that number will be odd, I shan't say oddness, but oneness,* and so on. See whether by now you have an adequate understanding of what I want.'

'Yes, quite adequate.'

'Answer then, and tell me what it is, by whose presence

10 in a body, that body will be living.'

'Soul.'

d   'And is that always so?'

'Of course.'

'Then soul, whatever it occupies, always comes to that thing bringing life?'

5   'It comes indeed.'

'And is there an opposite to life, or is there none?'

'There is.'

'What is it?'

'Death.'

10   'Now soul will absolutely never admit the opposite of what it brings up,* as has been agreed earlier?'

'Most emphatically,' said Cebes.

'Well now, what name did we give just now to what doesn't admit the form of the even?'

15   'Uneven.'

'And to that which doesn't admit the just, and to whatever doesn't admit the musical?'

e   'Unmusical, and unjust.'

'Well then, what do we call whatever doesn't admit death?'

'Immortal.'

'But soul doesn't admit death?'

'No.' 5

'Then soul is immortal.'

'It's immortal.'

'Very well. May we say that that much has been proved? Or how does it seem to you?'

'Yes, and very adequately proved, Socrates.'

'Now what about this, Cebes? If it were necessary for the 10 uneven to be imperishable, three would be imperishable, **106** wouldn't it?'

'Of course.'

'Or again, if the non-hot were necessarily imperishable likewise, then whenever anyone brought hot against snow, the snow would get out of the way, remaining intact and 5 unmelted? Because it couldn't perish, nor again could it abide and admit the heat.'

'True.'

'And in the same way, I imagine, if the non-coolable were imperishable, then whenever something cold attacked the fire, it could never be put out nor could it perish, but it 10 would depart and go away intact.'

'It would have to.'

'Then aren't we compelled to say the same thing about **b** the immortal? If the immortal is also imperishable, it's impossible for soul, whenever death attacks it, to perish. Because it follows from what's been said before that it won't admit death, nor will it be dead, just as we said that 5 three will not be even, any more than the odd will be; and again that fire will not be cold, any more than the heat in the fire will be. "But", someone might say, "what's to prevent the odd, instead of coming to be even, as we granted it didn't, when the even attacks, from perishing, **c** and there coming to be even in its place?" Against one who said that, we could not contend that it doesn't perish; because the uneven is not imperishable. If that had been granted us, we could easily have contended that when the 5 even attacks, the odd and three depart and go away. And we could have contended similarly about fire and hot and the rest, couldn't we?'

'Certainly we could.'

'So now, about the immortal likewise: if it's granted us
10 that it must also be imperishable, then soul, besides being
d immortal, would also be imperishable; but if not, another
argument would be needed.'

'But there's no need of one, on that score at least.
Because it could hardly be that anything else wouldn't
admit destruction if the immortal, being everlasting, is
going to admit destruction.'

5 'Well God anyway,' said Socrates, 'and the form of life
itself, and anything else immortal there may be, never
perish, as would, I think, be agreed by everyone.'

'Why yes, to be sure; by all human beings and still more,
I imagine, by gods.'

e 'Then, given that the immortal is also indestructible,
wouldn't soul, if it proves to be immortal, be imperishable
as well?'

'It absolutely must be imperishable.'

5 'Then when death attacks a person, the mortal part, it
seems, dies; whereas the immortal part gets out of the way
of death, departs, and goes away intact and undestroyed.'

'It appears so.'

'Beyond all doubt then, Cebes, soul is immortal and
107 imperishable, and our souls really will exist in Hades.'

'Well, Socrates, for my part I've no further objection, nor
can I doubt the arguments at any point. But if Simmias here
or anyone else has anything to say, he'd better not keep
5 silent; as I know of no future occasion to which anyone
wanting to speak or hear about such things could put it
off.'

'Well no,' said Simmias; 'nor have I any further ground
for doubt myself, as far as the arguments go; though in
b view of the size of the subject under discussion, and having
a low regard for human weakness, I'm bound to retain
some doubt in my mind about what's been said.'

'Not only that, Simmias,' said Socrates; 'what you say is
5 right, so the initial hypotheses,* even if they're acceptable
to you people, should still be examined more clearly: if you
analyse them adequately, you will, I believe, follow the
argument to the furthest point to which a human being can

follow it up; and if you get that clear, you'll seek nothing
further.'   10
   'What you say is true.'

   'But this much it's fair to keep in mind, friends: if a soul   c
is immortal, then it needs care, not only for the sake of this
time in which what we call "life" lasts, but for the whole of
time; and if anyone is going to neglect it, now the risk   5
would seem fearful. Because if death were a separation
from everything, it would be a godsend for the wicked,
when they died, to be separated at once from the body and
from their own wickedness along with the soul; but since,
in fact, it is evidently immortal, there would be no other   d
refuge from ills or salvation for it, except to become as
good and wise as possible. For the soul enters Hades taking
nothing else but its education and nurture, which are,
indeed, said to do the greatest benefit or harm to the one   5
who has died, at the very outset of his journey yonder.
   'Now it is said that when each one has died, the spirit
allotted to each in life proceeds to bring that individual to a
certain place, where those gathered must submit to
judgement, and then journey to Hades with the guide   e
appointed to conduct those in this world to the next; and
when they have experienced there the things they must, and
stayed there for the time required, another guide conveys
them back here during many long cycles of time. So the
journey is not as Aeschylus' Telephus* describes it; he says
it is a simple path that leads to Hades, but to me it seems to   108
be neither simple nor single. For then there would be no
need of guides; since no one, surely could lose the way
anywhere, if there were only a single road. But in fact it
probably has many forkings and branchings; I speak from   5
the evidence of the rites and observances followed here.*
Now the wise and well-ordered soul follows along, and is
not unfamiliar with what befalls it; but the soul in a state of
desire for the body, as I said earlier, flutters around it for a
long time, and around the region of the seen, and after   b
much resistance and many sufferings it goes along, brought
by force and against its will by the appointed spirit. And on

arriving where the others have gone, if the soul is
unpurified and has committed any such act as engaging in
5 wrongful killings, or performing such other deeds as may
be akin to those and the work of kindred souls, everyone
shuns and turns aside from it, and is unwilling to become
c its travelling companion or guide; but it wanders by itself
in a state of utter confusion, till certain periods of time
have elapsed, and when those have passed, it is taken
perforce into the dwelling meet for it; but the soul that has
passed through life with purity and moderation finds gods
5 for travelling companions and guides, and each inhabits
the region that befits it.

'Now there are many wondrous regions in the earth, and
the earth itself is of neither the nature nor the size supposed
by those who usually describe it, as someone has convinced
me.'

d Here Simmias said: 'What do you mean by that,
Socrates? I've heard many things about the earth too, but
not those that convince you; so I'd be glad to hear them.'

'Well, Simmias, I don't think the skill of Glaucus* is
5 needed to relate what they are; although to prove them true
does seem to me too hard for the skill of Glaucus—I
probably couldn't do it myself, and besides, even if I knew
how to, I think the life left me, Simmias, doesn't suffice for
e the length of the argument. Still, nothing prevents me from
telling of what I've been convinced the earth is like in
shape, and of its regions.'

'Well, even that is enough,' said Simmias.

'First then, I've been convinced that if it is round and in
5 the centre of the heaven, it needs neither air nor any other
109 such force to prevent its falling, but the uniformity of the
heaven in every direction with itself is enough to support it,
together with the equilibrium of the earth itself; because a
5 thing in equilibrium placed in the middle of something
uniform will be unable to incline either more or less in any
direction, but being in a uniform state it will remain
without incline. So that's the first thing of which I've been
convinced.'

'And rightly so,' said Simmias.

'And next, that it is of vast size, and that we who dwell between the Phasis River and the Pillars of Heracles* **b** inhabit only a small part of it, living around the sea like ants or frogs around a marsh, and that there are many others living elsewhere in many such places. For there are **5** many hollows all over the earth, varying in their shapes and sizes, into which water and mist and air have flowed together; and the earth itself is set in the heaven, a pure thing in pure surroundings, in which the stars are situated, and which most of those who usually describe such things **c** name "ether";* it's from that that these elements are the dregs, and continually flow together into the hollows of the earth. Now we ourselves are unaware that we live in its hollows, and think we live above the earth—just as if someone living at the bottom of the ocean were to think he **5** lived above the sea, and seeing the sun and the stars through the water, were to imagine that the sea was heaven, and yet through slowness and weakness had never **d** reached the surface of the sea, nor emerged, stuck his head up out of the sea into this region here, and seen how much purer and fairer it really is than their world, nor had heard this from anyone else who had seen it. Now that is just **5** what has happened to us: living in some hollow of the earth, we think we live above it, and we call the air "heaven", as if this were heaven and the stars moved through it; whereas the truth is just the same—because of **e** our weakness and slowness, we are unable to pass through to the summit of the air; for were anyone to go to its surface, or gain wings and fly aloft, he would stick his head up and see—just as here the fishes of the sea stick their **5** heads up and see the things here, so he would see the things up there; and if his nature were able to bear the vision, he would realize that that is the true heaven, the genuine light, **110** and the true earth. For this earth of ours, and its stones and all the region here, are corrupted and eaten away, as are things in the sea by the brine; nor does anything worth mentioning grow in the sea, and practically nothing is **5** perfect, but there are eroded rocks and sand and unimaginable mud and mire, wherever there is earth as well, and things are in no way worthy to be compared with the beauties in our world. But those objects in their turn would be seen to surpass the things in our world by a far greater measure still; indeed, if it is proper to tell a tale, it's worth hearing, Simmias, what the things upon the earth and beneath the heaven are actually like.'

'Why yes, Socrates,' said Simmias, 'we'd be glad to hear that tale.'

'Well then, my friend, first of all the true earth, if one views it from above, is said to look like those twelve-piece leather balls,* variegated, a patchwork of colours, of which our colours here are, as it were, samples that painters use. There the whole earth is of such colours, indeed of colours far brighter still and purer than these: one portion is purple, marvellous for its beauty, another is golden, and all that is white is whiter than chalk or snow; and the earth is composed of the other colours likewise, indeed of colours more numerous and beautiful than any we have seen. Even its very hollows, full as they are of water and air, give an appearance of colour, gleaming among the variety of the other colours, so that its general appearance is of one continuous multi-coloured surface. That being its nature, things that grow on it, trees and flowers and fruit, grow in proportion; and again, the mountains contain stones likewise, whose smoothness, transparency, and beauty of colour are in the same proportion; it is from those that the little stones we value, sardian stones, jaspers, emeralds, and all such, are pieces; but there, every single one is like that, or even more beautiful still. That is because the stones there are pure, and not corroded or corrupted, like those here, by mildew and brine due to the elements that have flowed together, bringing ugliness and disease to stones and earth, and to plants and animals as well. But the true earth is adorned with all these things, and with gold and silver also, and with the other things of that kind as well. For they are plainly visible, being many in number, large, and everywhere upon the earth; happy, therefore, are they who behold the sight of it. Among many other living things

upon it there are human beings, some dwelling inland, 5
some living by the air, as we live by the sea, and some on
islands surrounded by the air and lying close to the
mainland; and in a word, what the water and the sea are to
us for our needs, the air is to them; and what air is for us, b
ether is for them. Their climate is such that they are free
from sickness and live a far longer time than people here,
and they surpass us in sight, hearing, wisdom, and all such
faculties, by the extent to which air surpasses water for its 5
purity, and ether surpasses air. Moreover, they have groves
and temples of gods, in which gods are truly dwellers, and
utterances and prophecies, and direct awareness of the
gods; and communion of that kind they experience face to c
face. The sun and moon and stars are seen by them as they
really are, and their happiness in all else accords with that.

'Such is the nature of the earth as a whole and its surroundings; but in it there are many regions within the hollows it 5
has all around it, some deeper and some more extended
than the one in which we dwell, some deeper but with a
narrower opening than our own region, and others that are d
shallower in depth but broader than this one. All these are
interconnected underground in every direction, by passages
both narrower and wider, and they have channels through
which abundant water flows from one into another, as into 5
mixing bowls, and continuous underground rivers of
unimaginable size, with waters hot and cold, and abundant
fire and great rivers of fire, and many of liquid mud, some
purer and some more miry, like the rivers of mud in Sicily e
that flow ahead of the lava-stream, and the lava-stream
itself; with these each of the regions is filled, as the circling
stream happens to reach each one on each occasion. All of
this is kept moving back and forth by a kind of pulsation
going on within the earth; and the nature of this pulsation 5
is something like this: one of the openings in the earth
happens to be especially large, and perforated right 112
through the earth; it is this that Homer spoke of as:

A great way off, where lies the deepest pit beneath earth;*

and it is this that he and many other poets have elsewhere

5 called Tartarus. Now into this opening all the rivers flow
together, and from it they flow out again; and each
acquires its character from the nature of the earth through
b which it flows. The reason why all the streams flow out
there, and flow in, is that this liquid has neither bottom nor
resting place. So it pulsates and surges back and forth, and
the air and the breath enveloping it do the same; because
5 they follow it, when it rushes towards those areas of the
earth and again when it returns to these; and just as in
breathing the current of breath is continuously exhaled and
inhaled, so there the breath pulsating together with the
c liquid causes terrible and unimaginable winds, as it passes
in and out. Now when the water recedes into the so-called
"downward" region, it flows along the courses of those
streams through the earth and fills them, as in the process
of irrigation; and when it leaves there again and rushes
5 back here, then it fills these ones here once more; these,
when filled, flow through the channels and through the
earth, and reaching the regions into which a way has been
d made for each, they make seas and lakes and rivers and
springs; and then dipping again beneath the earth, some
circling longer and more numerous regions, and others
fewer and shorter ones, they discharge once more into
Tartarus, some a long way and others a little below where
5 the irrigation began; but all flow in below the point of
outflow, some across from where they poured out, and
some in the same part; and there are some that go right
round in a circle, coiling once or even many times around
the earth like serpents, and then, after descending as far as
e possible, discharge once more. It is possible to descend in
either direction as far as the middle but no further; because
the part on either side slopes uphill for both sets of streams.
    'Now there are many large streams of every kind; but
5 among their number there happen to be four in particular,
the largest of which, flowing outermost and round in a
circle, is the one called Oceanus; across from this and
113 flowing in the opposite direction is Acheron, which flows
through other desert regions, and in particular, flowing
underground, reaches the Acherusian Lake, where the

souls of most of those who have died arrive, and where, after they have stayed for certain appointed periods, some longer, some shorter, they are sent forth again into the generation of living things. The third river issues between these two, and near the point of issue it pours into a huge region all ablaze with fire, and forms a lake larger than our own sea, boiling with water and mud; from there it proceeds in a circle, turbid and muddy, and coiling about within the earth it reaches the borders of the Acherusian Lake, amongst other places, but does not mingle with its water; then, after repeated coiling underground, it discharges lower down in Tartarus; that is the river they name Pyriphlegethon, and it is from this that the lava-streams blast fragments up at various points upon the earth. Across from this again issues the fourth river, first into a region terrible and wild, it is said, coloured bluish-grey all over, which they name the Stygian region, and the river as it discharges forms a lake, the Styx; when it has poured in there, and gained terrible powers in the water, it dips beneath the earth, coils round and proceeds in the opposite direction to Pyriphlegethon, which it encounters in the Acherusian lake from the opposite side; nor does the water of that river mingle with any other, but it too goes round in a circle and discharges into Tartarus opposite to Pyriphlegethon; and its name, according to the poets, is Cocytus.

'Such, then, is their nature. Now when those who have died arrive at the region to which the spirit conveys each one, they first submit to judgement, both those who have lived honourable and holy lives and those who have not. Those who are found to have lived indifferently journey to Acheron, embark upon certain vessels provided for them, and on these they reach the lake; there they dwell, undergoing purgation by paying the penalty for their wrongdoings, and are absolved, if any has committed any wrong, and they secure reward for their good deeds, each according to his desert; but all who are found to be incurable because of the magnitude of their offences, through having committed many grave acts of sacrilege, or

many wrongful and illegal acts of killing, or any other
5 deeds that may be of that sort, are hurled by the
appropriate destiny into Tartarus, whence they nevermore
emerge. Those, again, who are found guilty of curable yet
114 grave offences, such as an act of violence in anger against a
father or a mother, and have lived the rest of their lives in
penitence, or who have committed homicide in some other
such fashion, must fall into Tartarus; and when they have
fallen and stayed there for a year, the surge casts them
5 forth, the homicides by way of Cocytus, and those who
have assaulted father or mother by way of Pyriphlegethon;
then, as they are carried along and draw level with the
Acherusian lake, they cry out and call, some to those they
b killed, others to those they injured; calling upon them, they
beg and beseech them to allow them to come forth into the
lake and to receive them; and if they persuade them, they
come forth and cease from their woes; but if not, they are
carried back into Tartarus, and from there again into the
5 rivers, and they do not cease from those sufferings till they
persuade those they have wronged; for that is the penalty
imposed upon them by their judges. But as for those who
are found to have lived exceptionally holy lives, it is they
who are freed and delivered from those regions within the
c earth, as from prisons, and who attain to the pure dwelling
above, and make their dwelling above ground. And among
their number, those who have been adequately purified by
philosophy live bodiless for the whole of time to come, and
attain to dwelling places fairer even than those, which it is
5 not easy to reveal, nor is the time sufficient at present. But
it is for the sake of just the things we have related, Simmias,
that one must do everything possible to have part in
goodness and wisdom during life; for fair is the prize and
great the hope.

d   'Now to insist that those things are just as I've related
them would not be fitting for a man of intelligence; but
that either that or something like it is true about our souls
and their dwellings, given that the soul evidently is
5 immortal, that, I think, is fitting and worth risking, for one
who believes that it is so—for a noble risk it is—so one

should repeat such things to oneself like a spell; which is
just why I've so prolonged the tale. For those reasons, then,
any man should have confidence for his own soul, who   e
during his life has rejected the pleasures of the body and its
adornments as alien, thinking they do more harm than
good, but has devoted himself to the pleasures of learning,   5
and has decked his soul with no alien adornment, but with 115
its own, with temperance and justice, bravery, liberality,
and truth, thus awaiting the journey he will make to
Hades, whenever destiny shall summon him. Now as for
you, Simmias and Cebes and the rest, you will make your
several journeys at some future time, but for myself, "e'en
now", as a tragic hero might say, "destiny doth summon   5
me"; and it's just about time I made for the bath: it really
seems better to take a bath before drinking the poison, and
not to give the women the trouble of washing a dead body.'

When he'd spoken, Crito said: 'Very well, Socrates: b
what instructions have you for these others or for me,
about your children or about anything else? What could we
do, that would be of most service to you?'

'What I'm always telling you, Crito,' said he, 'and   5
nothing very new: if you take care for yourselves, your
actions will be of service to me and mine, and to yourselves
too, whatever they may be, even if you make no promises
now; but if you take no care for yourselves, and are
unwilling to pursue your lives along the tracks, as it were,
marked by our present and earlier discussions, then even if   10
you make many firm promises at this time, you'll do no   c
good at all.'

'Then we'll strive to do as you say,' he said; 'but in what
fashion are we to bury you?'

'However you wish,' said he; 'provided you catch me,
that is, and I don't get away from you.' And with this he   5
laughed quietly, looked towards us and said: 'Friends, I
can't persuade Crito that I am Socrates here, the one who is
now conversing and arranging each of the things being
discussed; but he imagines I'm that dead body* he'll see in   d
a little while, so he goes and asks how he's to bury me! But

as for the great case I've been arguing all this time, that
when I drink the poison, I shall no longer remain with you,
but shall go off and depart for some happy state of the
5 blessed, this, I think, I'm putting to him in vain, while
comforting you and myself alike. So please stand surety for
me with Crito, the opposite surety to that which he stood
for me with the judges: his guarantee was that I would stay
behind, whereas you must guarantee that, when I die, I
shall not stay behind, but shall go off and depart; then
e Crito will bear it more easily, and when he sees the burning
or interment of my body, he won't be distressed for me, as
if I were suffering dreadful things, and won't say at the
funeral that it is Socrates they are laying out or bearing to
5 the grave or interring. Because you can be sure, my dear
Crito, that misuse of words* is not only troublesome in
itself, but actually has a bad effect on the soul. Rather, you
should be of good cheer, and say you are burying my body;
116 and bury it however you please, and think most proper.'

After saying this, he rose and went into a room to take a
bath, and Crito followed him but told us to wait. So we
waited, talking among ourselves about what had been said
5 and reviewing it, and then again dwelling on how great a
misfortune had befallen us, simply thinking of it as if we
were deprived of a father and would lead the rest of our life
b as orphans. After he'd bathed and his children had been
brought to him—he had two little sons and one big one—
and those women of his household had come, he talked
with them in Crito's presence, and gave certain directions
5 as to his wishes; he then told the women and children to
leave, and himself returned to us.

By now it was close to sunset, as he'd spent a long time
inside. So he came and sat down, fresh from his bath, and
there wasn't much talk after that. Then the prison official
c came in, stepped up to him and said, 'Socrates, I shan't
reproach you as I reproach others for being angry with me
and cursing, whenever by order of the rulers I direct them
5 to drink the poison. In your time here I've known you for
the most generous and gentlest and best of men who have
ever come to this place; and now especially, I feel sure it

isn't with me that you're angry, but with others, because you know who are responsible. Well now, you know the message I've come to bring: goodbye, then, and try to bear   d
the inevitable as easily as you can.' And with this he turned away in tears, and went off.

Socrates looked up at him and said: 'Goodbye to you too, and we'll do as you say.' And to us he added: 'What a   5
civil man he is! Throughout my time here he's been to see me, and sometimes talked with me, and been the best of fellows; and now how generous of him to weep for me! But come on, Crito, let's obey him: let someone bring in the poison, if it has been prepared; if not, let the man prepare it.'

Crito said: 'But Socrates, I think the sun is still on the   e
mountains and hasn't yet gone down. And besides, I know of others who've taken the draught long after the order had been given them, and after dining well and drinking plenty, and even in some cases enjoying themselves with those they   5
fancied. Be in no hurry, then: there's still time left.'

Socrates said: 'It's reasonable for those you speak of to do those things—because they think they gain by doing them; for myself, it's reasonable not to do them; because I think I'll gain nothing by taking the draught a little later: 117
I'll only earn my own ridicule by clinging to life, and being sparing when there's nothing more left. Go on now; do as I ask, and nothing else.'

Hearing this, Crito nodded to the boy who was standing nearby. The boy went out, and after spending a long time   5
away he returned, bringing the man who was going to administer the poison, and was carrying it ready-pounded in a cup.* When he saw the man, Socrates said: 'Well, my friend, you're an expert in these things: what must one do?'

'Simply drink it,' he said, 'and walk about till a heaviness comes over your legs; then lie down, and it will act of   b
itself.' And with this he held out the cup to Socrates.

He took it perfectly calmly, Echecrates, without a tremor, or any change of colour or countenance; but looking up at the man, and fixing him with his customary   5 stare, he said: 'What do you say to pouring someone a libation from this drink? Is it allowed or not?'

'We only prepare as much as we judge the proper dose, Socrates,' he said.

c   'I understand,' he said; 'but at least one may pray to the gods, and so one should, that the removal from this world to the next will be a happy one; that is my own prayer: so may it be.' With these words he pressed the cup to his lips, and drank it off with good humour and without the least distaste.

5   Till then most of us had been fairly well able to restrain our tears; but when we saw he was drinking, that he'd actually drunk it, we could do so no longer. In my own case, the tears came pouring out in spite of myself, so that I covered my face and wept for myself—not for him, no, but

d   for my own misfortune in being deprived of such a man for a companion. Even before me, Crito had moved away, when he was unable to restrain his tears. And Apollodorus, who even earlier had been continuously in tears, now burst

5   forth into such a storm of weeping and grieving, that he made everyone present break down except Socrates himself.

But Socrates said: 'What a way to behave, my strange friends! Why, it was mainly for that reason that I sent the

e   women away, so that they shouldn't make this sort of trouble; in fact, I've heard one should die in silence. Come now, calm yourselves and have strength.'

When we heard this, we were ashamed and checked our tears. He walked about, and when he said that his legs felt

5   heavy he lay down on his back—as the man told him—and then the man, this one who'd given him the poison, felt him, and after an interval examined his feet and legs; he then

118   pinched his foot hard and asked if he could feel it, and Socrates said not. After that he felt his shins once more; and moving upwards in this way, he showed us that he was becoming cold and numb. He went on feeling him, and said that when the coldness reached his heart, he would be gone.

5   By this time the coldness was somewhere in the region of his abdomen, when he uncovered his face—it had been

covered over—and spoke; and this was in fact his last
utterance: 'Crito,' he said 'we owe a cock to Asclepius:*
please pay the debt, and don't neglect it.'

'It shall be done,' said Crito; 'have you anything else to   10
say?'

To this question he made no answer, but after a short
interval he stirred, and when the man uncovered him his
eyes were fixed; when he saw this, Crito closed his mouth
and his eyes.

And that, Echecrates, was the end of our companion, a   15
man who, among those of his time we knew, was—so we
should say—the best, the wisest too, and the most just.

EXPLANATORY NOTES

57a   *Phaedo*: a close friend of Socrates, from Elis in the Peloponnese.
Little is known of him beyond what can be gathered from the
present dialogue. According to Diogenes Laertius (philosophical biographer of the third century AD), he was taken
captive by the Athenians, was ransomed at the instance of
Socrates, and thereafter practised philosophy 'as a free man'
(*Lives of the Philosophers*, ii. 105). It is not known why the
dialogue is named after him, but possibly it was he who gave
the original, first-hand account of Socrates' death to Plato
himself. See note on 60d.

  the poison: Athenian executions were carried out with juice
from the hemlock plant. The drug is not identified in the
Phaedo, but its use is well attested. It is expressly mentioned by
Xenophon, as used in an execution under the Thirty Tyrants
(*Hellenica*, ii. 3. 56). The drug worked by refrigeration (63d–e,
118a), but there is evidence that it could produce more violent
and distressing symptoms than those described in the final
scene of the *Phaedo*. Plato's account of Socrates' end may,
therefore, be carefully selective. See C. Gill, *Classical Quarterly*,
23 (1973), 25–8, and notes below on 63e, 117a.

  Echecrates: a Pythagorean philosopher. See Introduction,
pp. ix–x.

58b   *the famous 'seven pairs' . . . a mission to Delos*: the 'seven
pairs' were seven Athenian youths and maidens devoured
annually by the Minotaur, a man-eating monster kept by
Minos, king of Crete, and slain by Theseus. The small island of
Delos was sacred to the god Apollo.

59b   *Apollodorus—I think you know the man and his manner*: this
Apollodorus was notorious for his intense devotion to Socrates
and for his emotional volatility. See 117d. He appears in the
prologue to Plato's *Symposium*, where he is portrayed as a
fanatical convert to philosophy, 'always speaking ill of himself
and others' (173d).

  Critobulus and his father: Critobulus was well known for his
good looks. He appears in Xenophon's *Symposium*, where his
beauty and amorous susceptibility are subjects of banter (4.

10–28, 5. 1–10). Critobulus' father was Crito, Socrates' contemporary and one of his closest friends. Crito is Socrates' interlocutor in the Platonic dialogue named after him, and plays an important role in the dramatic action of the *Phaedo* (63d–e, 115b–118e).

Hermogenes: a member of the Socratic circle, who appears as one of Socrates' interlocutors in Plato's *Cratylus*.

Epigenes: mentioned in Plato's *Apology* (33e). Xenophon records a conversation between him and Socrates (*Memorabilia*, iii. 12).

Aeschines: a devotee of Socrates, who wrote speeches for the law-courts, taught oratory, and was admired as an author of Socratic dialogues. A few fragments of his writings are extant. His presence at Socrates' trial is noted in the *Apology* (33e).

Antisthenes: a dedicated follower of Socrates, according to Xenophon (*Symposium*, 8. 4–6, *Memorabilia*, iii. 11. 17). He was also the reputed founder of the eccentric philosophical sect known as the Cynics.

Ctesippus of the Paeanian deme: Ctesippus appears in Plato's *Lysis* and *Euthydemus*. A *deme* was one of the divisions, originally territorial, upon which the registration of Athenian citizens was based.

Menexenus: appears as a boy in the *Lysis* and as a young man in the minor Platonic work named after him.

Plato, I believe, was unwell: Plato's name occurs in his dialogues only in this passage and twice in the *Apology* (34a, 38b), where it is noted that he was present at Socrates' trial. Here, although Phaedo's account of Socrates' death has already been marked as first-hand (57a), Plato indicates that he did not witness it himself.

59c *Simmias of Thebes, and Cebes and Phaedondes*: Thebes was the chief city in Boeotia, about sixty kilometres north-west of Athens. Simmias and Cebes are mentioned in the *Crito* (45b), as having brought money to procure Socrates' escape from jail. Phaedondes is listed by Xenophon together with Simmias, Cebes, and other who associated with Socrates from unselfish motives and were of excellent character (*Memorabilia*, i. 2. 48).

Euclides and Terpsion from Megara: Megara was on the isthmus linking the Peloponnese with the rest of mainland Greece. Euclides was the head of a philosophical school there. He and Terpsion appear as speakers of the prologue to Plato's *Theaetetus*.

Aristippus: a companion of Socrates from Cyrene, with a reputation for a hedonistic lifestyle, and the traditional founder of the Cyrenaic school of philosophy. Its doctrine, that the pleasure of the moment is the only end of life, seems to have been formulated by his grandson of the same name. Diogenes Laertius (iii. 36) takes the present passage as a criticism of Aristippus, but Aristippus' absence may have been accidental, and may be recorded here, like Plato's own (59b), simply as a matter of fact.

Cleombrotus: according to an epigram by Callimachus (third century BC), a certain Cleombrotus of Ambracia threw himself into the sea after reading the *Phaedo*. See Cicero, *Tusculan Disputations*, i. 84. It is not known, however, whether the Cleombrotus who committed suicide was the one mentioned here.

Aegina: an island in the Saronic Gulf, about thirty kilometres south-west of Athens.

59e *the Eleven*: the prison commissioners responsible for state executions. See also *eleven Athenian gentlemen* at 85b. The prison official mentioned at 116b–c was their subordinate.

60a *Xanthippe . . . holding his little boy*: Xanthippe was Socrates' wife, the only one mentioned by Plato and Xenophon, though there is some indication that he had been previously married (Diogenes Laertius, ii. 26). He had three sons (116b, *Apology* 34d): two little boys, Sophroniscus and Menexenus, and an older one, Lamprocles. According to later tradition (Diogenes Laertius, ii. 36–7), Xanthippe was a most difficult woman. Xenophon makes Lamprocles say that 'no one could endure her bad temper' (*Memorabilia*, ii. 2. 7). He also makes Antisthenes say that she was 'the most bad-tempered of all women, past, present or future' (*Symposium*, 2. 10). Her present outburst is, however, perfectly natural for an emotionally charged occasion, and lends the tradition no support.

60b *this state that people call . . . visit a person together*: Greek has separate words for 'adult human male' (*anēr*) and 'member

82

of the human race' (*anthrōpos*). The latter has generally been translated 'human being' or 'person' (plural 'people'), but occasionally (e.g. 117a–b, 117e5) 'man' is unavoidable, as are masculine pronouns in many places where the word occurs in the singular.

60c   *God wanted to reconcile them*: a capital initial has sometimes been used for 'god' in the translation, although Plato's noun is not used, like the English 'God', as the proper name of a unique deity. The singular often occurs in the context of polytheistic belief (e.g. 58b, 61a–b, 85b), and Plato can shift rapidly between 'god' and 'gods' (e.g. 62b–d, 106d). Nevertheless, a capital is appropriate in passages whose tenor is monotheistic (e.g. 67a, 69d, 80d).

  now the pleasant seems to have come to succeed it: 'the pleasant' translates the definite article followed by an adjective. Such phrases are common in Greek, and are sometimes ambiguous, since they may refer either to a property or to that which possesses it. They may also signify the word used for the property in question, and so occasionally need to be rendered with quotation marks, e.g. 'painful' at 60b. See also notes on 70e, 103a.

60d   *including Evenus just the other day*: Evenus, from the island of Paros, is mentioned in the *Apology* (20a–b) as a professional teacher of human excellence or 'sophist'. As in that passage, considerable irony can be heard at 61b–c below, where it is insinuated that, unlike Socrates, he is concerned with worldly success, and is therefore no true philosopher.

  putting the tales of Aesop into verse: Aesop, to whom the body of Greek fable was traditionally ascribed, was a slave according to the fifth-century historian Herodotus (ii. 134). So, according to later tradition, was Phaedo (see note on 57a). It may not be too fanciful to see a parallel between Socrates using Aesop's tales as a basis for his verse compositions, and Plato using the story of Socrates' death, perhaps first told to him by Phaedo, as the basis for composition of our dialogue.

60e   *the same dream*: in accordance with archaic Greek belief, Socrates identifies his dream with a figure which visits the sleeper, speaks to him, and can even change its guise from one appearance to another.

83

61b *a poet should . . . make tales rather than true stories*: The Greek for 'poet' (*poiētēs*) means 'maker', and 'poetic' composition is here associated with 'making up' tales or imaginative fictions (*muthoi*), as opposed to stating truths in literal terms (*logoi*). Compare *Protagoras* (320c–328c), where the speaker begins with a fable and later (324d) shifts to explicit reasoned argument. Plato's combination of modes in the *Phaedo* is characteristic, marking him as both 'poet' and philosopher. See note on 70b and Introduction, p. xxi.

61d *Philolaus*: an influential fifth-century Pythagorean philosopher from Croton in southern Italy, who spent time in Thebes. See Introduction, p. x. A number of extant fragments are attributed to him, though their authenticity has been doubted.

62a *if this alone of all rules is unqualified*: this sentence is much vexed. The translation takes 'this' to refer to the supposition that death is never preferable to life. Socrates thinks that Cebes would reject that supposition, and would therefore question the teaching that suicide is never permissible. Many other interpretations are, however, possible.

62b *mysteries on the subject*: 'mysteries' were secret cults, requiring those who entered them to undergo rites of initiation. The teaching referred to here, like the initiations mentioned at 69c, is generally thought to have derived from the archaic religious movement known as Orphism.

we human beings are in some sort of prison: the translation 'prison' suits the theme of the soul's imprisonment in the body, which runs through the dialogue and is symbolized in its dramatic setting. The noun can also mean 'guardhouse', and if that is the meaning here, the thought is that the incarnate soul is on sentry duty, and that suicide is desertion of its post.

63e *one must bring nothing of that sort in contact with the poison*: i.e. one must not counteract the poison with anything that would heat the body. Because of its heating effect, wine was a recognized antidote to hemlock. See *Lysis*, 219e, and also *Historia Naturalis* by the elder Pliny (first century AD), xiv. 7. The executioner is anxious, as again at 117b, that there be enough poison for his purpose. Plutarch (first century AD) tells a bizarre story of an execution in which the supply of hemlock ran out, and the executioner refused to prepare any more until he was paid extra (*Life of Phocion*, ch. 36).

64a *dying and being dead*: Socrates will later (71a–72a) draw a distinction between the process of dying and the state of being dead.

64b *our own countrymen would quite agree*: the people of Boeotia were notoriously boorish, and Simmias' worldly fellow Thebans would have regarded the life of philosophers with pitying contempt.

64c *it is nothing but the separation of the soul from the body*: with this definition of death, Socrates assumes the dualistic view of soul and body that is fundamental for the whole dialogue. Compare 79b and see Introduction, pp. xv–xviii.

65b *aren't even the poets ... accurately?*: Plato may not have specific poets in mind. He is alluding to a general tendency to disparage the senses in favour of the intellect, which had marked Greek philosophy from its earliest stages. For the 'deceitfulness' of the senses, see also 83a–b. It consists not merely in well-known illusions or weaknesses of the senses, but in their shutting out awareness of all realities other than those of the sensible world.

when does the soul attain the truth?: here and throughout the following passage (65c–68b) the soul is conceived as pure intellect or reason. See Introduction, p. xvi.

65d *that a just itself is a reality ... a beautiful and a good*: the first appearance in the *Phaedo* of 'forms', conceived as objects of purely intellectual understanding. Here, as often, they are designated by simple adjectives. See also 74a–77a, 100a–101c, with notes, and Introduction, pp. x–xv.

66c *as the saying goes*: the saying or proverb referred to is unknown.

68a *of human loves, of wives and sons*: 'human loves' are boy-loves (*paidika*). There may be an implied contrast between the objects of male homosexual passion and wisdom as the object of the philosopher's desire. Compare Plato's *Gorgias* 482a, where Socrates calls philosophy his *paidika*. 'Wives and sons' cannot be examples of *paidika*, and the words have therefore been suspected as an interpolation into the text. A descent into Hades in quest of a deceased wife does, however, occur in the story of Orpheus, which is referred to by Plato in the *Symposium* (179d).

68b *a lover of wisdom*: elsewhere the word *philosophos* has been translated 'philosopher', but its literal meaning needs to be brought out here to mark the contrast with other sorts of 'lover' at 68c. The philosopher is one who aspires to wisdom but has not yet attained it. See 66e–67a and *Symposium*, 204a–c.

68c *what is named "bravery"*: what is ordinarily called 'bravery' is misnamed, since it involves only an intelligent calculation of self-interest. For the same reason 'temperance' in the ordinary sense is a misnomer (68e). It is only the philosopher who exhibits 'true' bravery, temperance, and other virtues (69b).

68d *brave through fear and cowardice*: it is paradoxical that anything should possess a quality by reason of the opposite of that quality. Similarly, temperate people, ordinarily so called, 'achieve temperance because of intemperance' (69a), hence they cannot be truly temperate. Later stretches of argument will rely on the same principle (94a, 100b–101b).

69b *bravery, temperance, justice, … wisdom*: this quartet of virtues appears together in various Platonic contexts, notably in *Republic*, Book iv, where they provide a framework for the definition of justice. They later became entrenched in Christian moral teaching as the four 'cardinal' virtues. For their role in Plato's ethics, see F. E. Sparshott, *The Monist*, 55 (1970), 40–65.

69c *lie in the slough*: part of punishment in the afterlife according to Orphic teaching. In the *Republic* (363d) those who exploited such teaching, by playing upon the superstitious fear of punishment in the next world, are treated by Plato with withering contempt.

69d *"many who bear the wand, but few who are devotees"*: a wand was carried by the Bacchanals or worshippers of the god Dionysus. 'Bearing the wand' here represents the mere performance of ritual, as distinct from true religious devotion.

70b *Would you like us to speculate*: literally 'to tell a tale'. The verb is compounded from the Greek roots of the English 'myth' and 'logic', and is well suited to the arguments for immortality which follow. Earlier (61b) Socrates has declared that he is 'no teller of tales'; but in his arguments, as in the whole dialogue, logic and myth are continually interwoven. See Introduction, p. xxi.

70c *even if he were a comic poet*: the reference is probably to Aristophanes' *Clouds*, first produced in 423 BC, where Socrates is caricatured as a purveyor of newfangled thinking, sterile logic-chopping, and pseudo-science. As if in answer to the charge that philosophy has 'nothing to do with real life', Plato repeatedly brings out the connection between Socrates' present inquiry and his 'real life' situation (76b, 78a, 80d, 84c–85b, 89b, 91a–c, 98c–99a, 115b).

an ancient doctrine, which we've recalled: Socrates glances back to his earlier references to religious teachings about the afterlife (63c, 69c). The 'ancient doctrine' of reincarnation may be of Orphic origin. It is attested as Pythagorean, and was also affirmed by the fifth-century Sicilian philosopher, Empedocles.

70e *all things subject to coming-to-be*: the noun translated 'coming-to-be' (*genesis*) covers at least two notions that are less clearly distinct in Greek than in English: (*a*) the coming into existence of what did not previously exist, and (*b*) the process whereby an existing object becomes what it previously was not, i.e. undergoes change. The same noun and its cognate verb, when used of living things, can also mean 'birth' and 'be born', and have often been so translated in what follows. In particular, they are used of the soul's being 'born into', or becoming incarnate in, the body.

the beautiful is opposite, of course, to the ugly: expressions such as 'the beautiful' and 'the ugly' may mean either the properties of beauty and ugliness or the things that possess those properties. The ambiguity will be recognized as a source of difficulty later (103a–b), with reference back to the present passage. See notes on 60c, 103a.

71b *even if in some cases we don't use the names*: this could mean either (*a*) 'there are some processes for which names are lacking', or (*b*) 'we don't use the name "coming-to-be" for every process to which, properly speaking, it applies'. At 71e 'dying', for example, will be treated as a 'coming-to-be', yet in ordinary usage it would not be so called.

72a *Then look at it this way*: the detail of the following argument is obscure, but its main point is to posit a process of 'coming to life again', in order to ensure that life and change continue to occur in the universe for ever. Plato's view of the universe is organic. In his *Timaeus* he compares it with an ever-living animal.

72c *Endymion*: a mythical figure who was loved by the goddess of the moon and granted everlasting sleep.

Anaxagoras' notion of "all things together" would soon be realized: Anaxagoras was an important fifth-century philosopher, originally from Clazomenae in Ionia. He spent many years in Athens and was prominent in Athenian intellectual life. Fragments of his work are extant. According to one tradition, he was prosecuted for heresies regarding the composition of the sun and moon. In the *Apology* (26d) Socrates ridicules the charge that he had expounded Anaxagoras' views, noting that the philosopher's own book was easily available. Anaxagoras' idea that all things are ordered by a cosmic intelligence will come in for scathing criticism later. See 97c with note. The present passage refers to his idea that all elements in the universe were once completely intermingled. That state of affairs would soon come about once again, Socrates argues, if dying were not complemented by a process of coming to life.

72d *if the living things came to be from the other things*: it is unclear what are 'the other things' from which living things are supposed to come. They may be 'things other than the living', i.e. non-living sources which might eventually be exhausted, so that everything would end up dead.

72e *our learning is actually nothing but recollection*: the noun translated 'recollection' (*anamnēsis*) is cognate with the verb for 'to be reminded'. Neither noun nor verb is limited in ordinary usage to being reminded of an already familiar object by perceiving something else. As Simmias' joking use of the verb (73b) shows, it also covers verbal prompting by another person of a truth known but forgotten. For the Platonic doctrine of 'recollection' see Introduction, pp. xviii–xx.

73a *so in this way too, it appears that the soul is something immortal*: 'immortality' is not restricted to the soul's existence after death, but includes its existence before birth (or conception). These two aspects of immortality will be brought together at 77b–d.

when people are questioned . . . they state the truth about everything for themselves: possibly an allusion to *Meno*

81e–86b. See Introduction, p. xix, and G. Vlastos, *Dialogue*, 4 (1965), 143–57.

73d *someone seeing Simmias is often reminded of Cebes*: presumably because of their close association in the Theban philosophical community.

74a *we say ... that there is something that is equal*: this refers to the Platonic form of equality. It has been translated in the following passage as 'the equal itself', or 'equality', or 'that thing which equal is'. A crucial argument to distinguish it from its sensible instances follows immediately (74b–c). The argument is extended to a wider range of forms at 75c–d. See note on 75d, and Introduction, pp. x–xv.

74b *aren't equal stones and logs ... evidently ...?*: this question could also be translated: 'don't equal stones and logs ... sometimes seem equal to one but not to another?' Similarly, Socrates' next question could be translated: 'did the equals themselves ever seem to you unequal, or equality inequality?' The Greek verb is ambiguous between 'seem' and 'evidently be'. The latter has been preferred here because it gives Socrates a stronger argument. For if sensible equals were merely to seem unequal without actually being so, no real distinction between them and the form of equality would have been established.

equal to one, but not to another: the meaning may be either (*a*) 'equal to one person but not to another', or (*b*) 'equal to one thing but not to another'. On interpretation (*a*) judgements concerning the equality of sensible objects are thought of as subjective. On interpretation (*b*) they are thought of as relative. With a variant manuscript reading, the meaning will be (*c*) 'equal at one time but not at another'.

74c *the equals themselves*: this plural phrase has been much discussed. Some have taken it to refer to abstract mathematical equals, such as the angles at the base of an isosceles triangle. These, however, have no obvious relevance to the context, and their introduction here would destroy the logic of the argument. The phrase is better understood as an alternative designation for the form of equality, used as a variant for 'the equal itself'. Despite its plural form, the phrase need not be plural in meaning, as shown by A. Teffeteller Dale, *American Journal of Philology*, 108 (1987), 384–99.

75a *striving to be like the equal*: for the supposed implications of this phrase, see Introduction, p. xiii.

75d *it concerns everything on which we set this seal, "that which it is"*: the argument extends to all items 'stamped' by the terminology for forms. That terminology originates from questions such as 'what is beauty?' or 'what is justice?' Platonic forms are objects that provide answers to those questions. The present phrase might be glossed as 'that which X is', answering the question, 'what is X?' For the connection of terminology for forms with questions and answers, see also 78d with note, and Introduction, p. xii.

76e *finding again what was formerly ours*: i.e. recovering knowledge of the forms which we possessed prenatally.

our souls exist: literally 'our soul exists'. Here, and below (77a–c), 'soul' occurs in the singular, but it carries no suggestion of a single 'collective soul' for the human race, or 'cosmic soul' for the universe as a whole. The present argument, like the entire dialogue, is concerned with the survival of the souls of individuals. Occasionally, however, where 'soul' occurs in the singular without a definite article (e.g. 79e–80b, 105c–e), it may be thought of generically, as a kind of incorporeal stuff, distinguishable from individual souls, as 'body' in the sense of 'matter' is distinguishable from individual bodies.

78d *the reality itself, whose being we give an account of in asking and answering questions*: 'the reality itself', refers to the domain of forms; 'whose being we give an account of' could mean either (*a*) 'whose essential nature we define', or (*b*) 'whose existence we prove'. The reference to 'asking and answering questions', which suggests a connection with the philosopher's search for definitions, makes (*a*) more likely. See note on 75d.

79b *we ourselves are part body and part soul*: for the dualistic assumption, see Introduction, p. xvii.

80d *"Hades" in the true sense of the word*: the realm of 'Hades', i.e. the underworld, is linked to the word for 'unseen' (*aides*) by a doubtful etymology, which is rejected in the *Cratylus* (404b). The domain of forms is called 'Hades in the true sense', because it is not visible to the eye, but is an object of the intellect. Here, as elsewhere (58e, 68b), the traditional Greek view of Hades as a realm of gloom and shadow is transformed.

81e *whatever types of character they may have cultivated in their lifetime*: although the idea of reincarnation in animals is Pythagorean, the irony with which it is developed in this passage is Plato's own.

84a *the endless task of a Penelope working in reverse at a kind of web*: Penelope, wife of Odysseus, was wooed by suitors during the long absence of her husband at the Trojan War. She kept them at bay by promising them a decision when she had finished her weaving, and then unpicking, every night, the work she had done during the day. The soul is said to be working at her endless task 'in reverse', because, through sensual indulgence, it weaves again by night the 'web' that philosophy has unravelled by day.

not the object of opinion: this phrase, applied to the forms, glances at the important Platonic contrast between opinion (*doxa*) and knowledge (*epistēmē*). These mental states are differentiated in the *Republic* (476–80) according to their objects, forms being the domain of knowledge and sensible things the domain of opinion.

85b *eleven Athenian gentlemen*: see note on 59e.

85e *the attunement of a lyre and its strings*: the word translated 'attunement' (*harmonia*) is often given as 'harmony'. But the associations of that word in modern music are misleading, and the forthcoming argument will focus mainly upon the tuned state of the instrument. For the wider significance of the 'attunement' theory of the soul, see Introduction, p. xviii.

86b *what we actually take the soul to be*: In saying 'we', Simmias may be associating himself with 'many people' or 'people in general', since the attunement theory evidently had wide appeal (92d). He has sometimes been understood to mean 'we Pythagoreans', but his attunement theory is not easy to reconcile with Pythagorean ideas about the soul which underlie the prohibition of suicide (61e–62b) and the belief in reincarnation (82a–b).

89b *to make fun of my hair*: the meaning could be 'to play with my hair'. But if the translation is correct, Socrates may be making fun of Phaedo for wearing his hair long, even though he was past the age at which it was customary in Athens to do so. The cutting of hair was a sign of mourning.

89c *I should swear an oath, like the Argives*: according to Herodotus (i. 82), the people of Argos, after losing a city to the Spartans, shaved their heads and vowed not to let their hair grow again until they had recaptured it.

Heracles ... Iolaus: one of the labours of Heracles was to fight the Lenaean Hydra. During the fight Heracles was attacked by a large crab, and called his nephew Iolaus to his aid. See *Euthydemus* 297c.

89d *"misologists"*: the meaning of this word, coined from the Greek, is evident from the context. 'Misology' is intellectual defeatism, a general distrust of rational argument. For Socrates' warning against this attitude, and its implications for the philosophical spirit of the *Phaedo*, see Introduction, p. xxiii.

90c *those who've spent all their time on contradictory arguments*: practised disputants, who could construct plausible arguments both for and against any given proposition, and thereby bring all rational discussion into disrepute. Such a style of argument, aiming to score points rather than discover truth, was prevalent in Plato's Athens. Good specimens of it are preserved in an anonymous, late fifth-century treatise, *Dissoi Logoi* or 'Arguments Both Ways'. The 'contradiction-mongers' will be attacked again at 101e. Plato made fun of their activities in the *Euthydemus*, perceiving them as a threat to the dispassionate search for truth.

things fluctuating in the Euripus: the Euripus was the narrow channel separating the island of Euboea from mainland Greece. It was notorious for the strength and variability of its currents.

92d *just as surely as its object exists ... "that which it is"*: Simmias is referring back to 76e. For his terminology for the forms, see note on 75d.

93b *if it's been tuned more and to a greater extent ... more an attunement*: being tuned 'more' may refer to a more exact tuning of an individual lyre string, and being tuned 'to a greater extent' to the tuning of a greater number of strings. Nothing in the coming argument, however, turns upon the distinction.

93c *Are they, in turn, a further attunement and non-attunement?*:
it is suggested here that attunement is what distinguishes good
souls from bad ones. This is similar to the account of virtues
given in the *Republic* (430e, 443d–e), where temperance and
justice are defined in terms of 'attunement' within the soul and
the state. That account, however, is based upon a doctrine of
'parts' of the soul ('reason', 'spirit', and 'appetite') which must
be 'attuned' with one another. It fits less easily with the
Phaedo's view of the soul as non-composite, i.e. having no
parts (78c).

93d *but it's already been agreed . . . and this is the admission that
no one attunement is more . . . an attunement than another*:
the inference in the second half of this sentence depends upon
substituting 'attunement' for 'soul' in what has been agreed in
the first half. The substitution is, supposedly, warranted by the
identification of soul with attunement according to Simmias'
theory. By making the substitution, Socrates argues that the
theory leads to unacceptable consequences, reached at 94a.

94e *'Striking . . . endure'*: from Homer's *Odyssey*, xx. 17–18.

95a *the Theban lady Harmonia*: Harmonia was the wife of
Cadmus, legendary founder of Thebes. Socrates jokingly
identifies the Theban Simmias' theory with her, since it bears
her name (see note on 85e). The other Theban objection, that
of Cebes, is identified with Cadmus.

95b *some evil eye*: a malign influence affecting those who 'tempt
providence' by boasting.

95e *the reason*: in what follows Socrates will use 'reason' sometimes for the cause which makes a thing to be as it is, and
sometimes for the essential nature by virtue of which it is
whatever it is. His story thus ranges over two different sorts of
inquiry: the scientist's quest for causal explanation, and the
philosopher's quest for logical understanding. The use of
'reason' for both kinds of venture enables them to be
assimilated as well as contrasted.

96a *coming-to-be and destruction*: 'coming-to-be' can mean either
the coming into existence of what did not previously exist or
the acquisition by existent things of new properties (see note
on 70e). In the following narrative, whether or not it contains
any truth about the historical Socrates, Plato is exercised with
philosophical problems posed by the notions of birth and

change, death and destruction. His great fifth-century predecessor, the philosopher-poet Parmenides of Elea, had undercut scientific inquiry, by arguing, on purely logical grounds, that all coming-to-be and perishing were impossible. For how, he had asked, could 'what-is-not' ever 'be' or 'come to be'? And how could 'what-is' ever 'not be' or 'cease to be'? The difficulty of understanding coming-to-be or change of any sort, in face of the Parmenidean challenge, underlies much of Socrates' account of his intellectual development. See C. Stough, *Phronesis*, 21 (1976), 1–30.

96b *examining, for a start, questions like these*: questions concerning the origins of life, thought, perception, and memory, had all been subjects of speculation by Socrates' fifth-century predecessors. The theory mentioned about the origin of life may have been that of Archelaus, a pupil of Anaxagoras who is said to have taught Socrates. Although the brain had been held to be the seat of consciousness by Alcmaeon of Croton and also in Hippocratic medicine, its role was not generally recognized in antiquity. Theories attributing consciousness to blood, air, and fire had been held by Empedocles, Diogenes of Apollonia, and Heraclitus of Ephesus, respectively; Aristotle and the Stoics ascribed it to the heart. These scientific disagreements, however, were irrelevant to Socrates' concerns. He intimates that *all* merely physiological explanations of life and consciousness were, from a philosophical perspective, inadequate. He was led to renounce scientific inquiry altogether by his preoccupation with logical problems to which natural scientists (then as now) remained totally impervious.

96c *I was then so utterly blinded by this inquiry, that I unlearned even those things I formerly supposed I knew*: Compare 'I was afraid I might be completely blinded in my soul' (99e). Socrates' confession that he was 'blinded' by science is ironical. He pretends that even the simplest causal explanation, such as the attribution of human growth to the intake of food, was too hard for him. His problem in understanding growth could not be solved by a 'reason' of that sort. For it was the logical problem of understanding how growth, or any other sort of change, was possible at all. See notes on 96a and 96b.

96e *larger just by a head*: a head is, of course, neither a reason nor a cause of one person's being larger than another, but a measure of the difference between them. Plato is not, however, merely playing with words. He is using a trivial example to make a serious point: the difference in size between A and B is not what constitutes A's being 'larger' than B. The 'head' example will become crucial later (101a–b). See notes on 101b, 105c, 105d.

because of their exceeding the latter by half: sc. of themselves, i.e. by one cubit.

97a *Because I wonder if ... they were juxtaposed*: Socrates wonders how bringing two items together can make them 'come to be two'. For considered as a pair, they were two already, even before they were juxtaposed; and considered singly, each of them still remains one, even after they have been brought together. Compare G. Frege: 'Must we literally hold a rally of all the blind in Germany before we can attach any sense to the expression "the number of blind in Germany"?' (*The Foundations of Arithmetic*, sect. 23).

97b *we have a reason opposite to the previous one*: 'division' or 'splitting' is unacceptable as a reason for things' 'coming to be two', because it is the opposite of 'addition'. Two opposite processes cannot both function as 'reasons' (given Socrates' stringent criteria for acceptable 'reasons') why a subject should acquire one and the same property.

97c *Anaxagoras*: see note on 72c. Socrates' celebrated critique of Anaxagoras is a point of great moment for Western intellectual history. It marks the emergence of a mode of explanation which was to dominate European science for some two thousand years. Explanations of the physical world in terms of 'what is best', often called 'teleological' explanations, were developed by Plato in the *Timaeus*. They were fundamental in the thought of Aristotle, and became known traditionally as 'final causes'. Socrates' central point against Anaxagoras is that one who attributes the physical world to 'intelligence' is committed to showing how it exhibits purposive design. Yet Anaxagoras had utterly failed to do this.

98b *I beheld a man making no use of his intelligence at all*: Socrates slyly insinuates that Anaxagoras failed not only to invoke his theory of a cosmic intelligence, but also to use his own. A play on the word 'intelligence' has already occurred at 97d, 'an instructor ... to suit my own intelligence'.

99a *I dare swear*: literally 'by the dog', a favourite Socratic oath.

99b *feeling it over blindfold*: an allusion to blind man's buff. The
blindfold player, after catching one of the others, has to 'paw
him over' and try to guess his name correctly. It is with such a
player that Socrates compares most people in their misuse of
the term 'reason'.

a flat kneading-trough: a round utensil, illustrating the base of
air which supports the earth according to the theory that
Socrates is caricaturing.

99c *an Atlas stronger and more immortal than that*: Atlas was a
mythical Titan giant who held up the sky. Socrates mocks
scientific cosmology as being no less naïve, fundamentally,
than myth.

the good or binding: this is an explanation of the sort implied
by postulating intelligence as the reason for all things. See note
on 97c.

99d *my second voyage in quest of the reason*: the nature of
Socrates' 'second voyage' has been much debated. It is
uncertain whether he means 'taking to the oars when the wind
has failed', or 'making a second, safer journey' to whatever
port he had been trying to reach. His nautical metaphor and
tentative tone are in the same vein as Simmias' remarks at 85c–d,
and the language of the two passages is strikingly similar.
Compare also 66e–67a, and see K. M. W. Shipton, *Phronesis*,
24 (1979), 33–53.

99e *I thought I should take refuge in theories*: Socrates abandoned
scientific for philosophical inquiries, examining things by
seeking their definitions ('what is beauty?', 'what is justice?',
etc.) and using logical argument rather than sensory observation.
See notes on 75d, 78d, and Introduction, p. xii.

100a *I don't at all admit . . . examines them in concrete*: Socrates
qualifies his comparison (99d–e) of studying things through
their definitions with looking at things through their images.
He wishes to avoid any suggestion that definitions, as mere
images of the forms, are inferior to their concrete embodiments
in the physical world. Definitions, as products of philosophical
inquiry, are images on a higher level, for Plato, than objects in
the sensible world. To study reality through them is to come
closer to truth than is possible through empirical investigation.
See Introduction, p. xx.

100b *those much harped-on entities*: i.e. the forms. See notes on 65d, 74a, 74b, 75d, 76e, 78d, and Introduction, pp. x–xv.

100d *whatever the manner and nature of the relation may be*: Socrates leaves open the question of exactly how the relationship of the form of beauty to particular beautiful items is to be understood. The attempt to express this relationship with full philosophical rigour creates difficulties for the theory of forms. Some of these are explored by Plato in the first part of his *Parmenides*.

100e *by the beautiful*: less literally, 'by reason of', 'by virtue of'.

101a *the larger will be larger and the smaller smaller by the same thing*: Socrates may mean (*a*) that if X is larger than Y by a head, then Y is smaller than X by a head; hence two different items are larger and smaller than each other by the same amount. Or he may mean (*b*) that if X is larger than Y by a head and also smaller than Z by a head, then a single item (X) will be both larger and smaller by the same amount. Interpretation (*b*) fits better with the example introduced at 102b–d.

101b *it's surely monstrous that anyone should be large by something small*: i.e. the reason for a thing's having a certain property cannot itself possess the opposite of that property. This principle will be basic in the final argument for the soul's immortality. See notes on 105c, 105d.

101c *participation in twoness*: Plato uses two sets of terms for numbers: (1) the ordinary words for the cardinal number series; and (2) words formed upon those in (1) with a distinctive termination. The translation uses ordinary English numbers for the first series, and adds '-ness' to them for terms in the second. Sometimes (as here) terms in the second series are clearly being used for forms of the relevant numbers. But from 104a onwards the meaning of number words is often more debatable, and no systematic distinction seems intended between the two types of term.

101d *scared of your own shadow, as the saying is*: i.e. nervous, fearful of refutation by the 'contradiction-mongers'. The saying may have originated, like the English 'take umbrage', from horses shying at their shadows.

But if anyone fastened upon the hypothesis itself: the text and sense are uncertain. Socrates seems to be thinking of an objector who challenges the hypothesis as itself engendering serious contradictions. The theory of forms itself is beset by such difficulties in the *Parmenides*. See note on 100d, and Introduction, p. xv.

101e *positing another hypothesis, whichever should seem best of those above, till you came to something adequate*: Socrates seems to have in mind the positing of a second hypothesis from which the first one, when it has to be justified, can be seen to follow. 'Something adequate' could mean a proposition that the imagined objector is prepared to accept, or perhaps one that is no longer adopted merely as a provisional hypothesis, but is self-evidently true.

as the contradiction-mongers do: see note on 90c.

102b *both things are in Simmias, largeness and smallness*: Socrates reformulates the ordinary statement 'Simmias is larger than Socrates' in terms of the theory of forms, as a statement about Simmias' largeness in relation to Socrates' smallness. The use of 'large' and 'small' in ordinary judgements of magnitude must always be relative. Because Simmias exemplifies both largeness and smallness when viewed in relation to different things, he cannot be identified with either 'the large' or 'the small'. By contrast, the forms of largeness and smallness are large and small in a non-relative way, and can thus serve as the true bearers of the names 'large' and 'small'. Compare what was said of the form of equality, by contrast with equal logs and stones, at 74b–c. It remains far from obvious, however, exactly how the present reformulation is meant to be an improvement on the statement it replaces.

102c *Because it isn't, surely, by nature that Simmias overtops him, by virtue, that is, of his being Simmias*: with this example Plato adumbrates a distinction between a thing's 'essential' properties, i.e. those that it must possess by virtue of its very nature, and 'accidental' ones that it merely happens to possess and might lack without ceasing to be itself. Since Simmias would still be Simmias even if Socrates were to grow taller than he, his being taller than Socrates is not an 'essential' property, but a merely 'accidental' one. The distinction will be important for the argument below (103c–105e), where certain subjects are said to possess certain of their properties by their very nature. Heat and cold, oddness, and life, will be represented as essential properties of fire and snow, three, and soul, respectively.

102d *talk like a book*: Socrates compares his cumbersome style with that of a pedantic or jargon-ridden document, perhaps a legal or academic one.

but also that the largeness in us never admits the small: like the form of largeness, an individual person's largeness can never acquire the opposite property, smallness. The point of distinguishing the form from its manifestation 'in us' is hard to understand. Plato may have his eye on the coming argument for immortality. It needs to be proved that the soul *in each individual* will not admit death (88a–b, 91d, 95d, 107a). Perhaps, therefore, the refusal of 'the large in us' to admit smallness prefigures the refusal of 'the soul in us' to admit death.

102e *either it must retreat . . . or else, upon that opposite's advance, it must perish*: it is difficult to interpret Plato's military metaphors, 'advancing', 'retreating', and 'perishing', especially in connection with largeness and smallness. Perhaps Simmias' smallness is thought of as 'advancing' and his largeness as 'retreating' when he is compared with Phaedo, and conversely when he is compared with Socrates. By contrast, if he were to grow larger than Phaedo, then his smallness and Phaedo's largeness would 'perish'. 'Perishing' requires an actual change of size, whereas 'advancing' or 'retreating' requires only a shift of comparison.

103a *in our earlier discussion*: see 70e–71a with note. It is now recognized that expressions such as 'the large' can mean either (*a*) 'that which is large' or (*b*) 'largeness'. In sense (*a*) 'the large' can come to be small, whereas in sense (*b*) it cannot. By removing the ambiguity, Socrates can uphold the principle that 'opposites come from opposites' (71a), used in his first proof of immortality. The distinction between largeness and that which is large also helps to answer the problem of change posed by Parmenides. See notes on 60c, 96a.

103d *the hot is something different from fire, and the cold is something different from snow*: 'the hot' and 'the cold' are evidently thought of as forms of heat and cold. But it is uncertain, here and throughout the following argument, whether fire and snow are thought of as forms, or as ordinary substances in the physical world. The translation assumes the latter interpretation.

104a *Consider the case of threeness*: in Plato's elaboration of this example it is often uncertain whether the number three or the form of three is meant, and even whether any clear-cut distinction is envisaged between numbers and forms for numbers. See note on 101c.

104c *there are, in addition, certain other things that don't abide the opposites' attack*: some would translate 'there are, in addition, certain other forms that don't abide the opposites' attack'. This will be the sense, if it is correct to understand the class of things in question as a class of forms, exemplified by forms of fire and snow (see note on 103d). However, there is no word for 'forms' at this point in Plato's text.

104d *things that are compelled by whatever occupies them to have not only its own form, but always the form of some opposite as well*: alternatively, 'things that compel whatever they occupy to have not only its own character but the character of some opposite as well'. The choice between this and the translation adopted affects interpretation of the wider argument. With the alternative translation, the class of things Socrates is trying to define will be a class of occupying forms, such as the form of 'three' (104d). With the translation adopted, the things to be defined will be occupied by forms, and are therefore less likely to be forms themselves.

105a *nor will ten, its double, admit that of the odd*: these words are best understood as an aside about the term 'double'. Unlike terms in the ordinary number series, such as two, three, five, and ten, 'double' has an opposite (namely, 'half'): yet like the even members of the number series it excludes oddness, since no number that is double can be odd.

105b *one-and-a-half, and the rest of that series, the halves . . . a third, and all that series*: the two series referred to are 1/2, 3/2, 5/2, etc., and 1/3, 4/3, 7/3, etc. No term in either series will 'admit the whole', i.e. none can be a whole number. These further examples are of no importance for the main argument.

105c *a different kind of safety . . . the old safe, ignorant answer*: Socrates harks back to the reason given earlier (100b–d) why a given thing is beautiful, namely, the form of beauty. It was 'safe' (100d, 101c–d) because it escaped the contradictions engendered by other types of answer, and 'ignorant' because it was tautological. Socrates sees 'a different kind of safety' in the answer he will now give to the question why a thing is, for example, hot. The answer 'fire' is not a mere tautology, but is still 'safe'. For since fire is incapable of being cold, it can explain why a body is hot without contradiction. The general principle implicit in the 'subtler answers' given here is that whatever explains a given property must be incapable of possessing that property's opposite. See note on 101b.

I shan't say oddness, but oneness: see note on 101c. It is uncertain whether the form of oneness is meant, as at 101c, or 'a unit', i.e. the 'one' left over in the middle when an odd number is divided into equal parts. Such a unit, by its presence in any odd number, could be thought of as making that number odd.

105d *soul will absolutely never admit the opposite of what it brings up*: here the principle implicit in the examples at 105b–c is applied to soul. If soul is to be a 'reason' for life in a body, it cannot admit the opposite of life, namely, death.

107b *the initial hypotheses*: including, presumably, the hypotheses positing the existence of forms, upon which the case for immortality has so often rested (65d–e, 74a, 76d–e, 92d–e, 100a–101c).

107e *Aeschylus' Telephus*: an allusion to a lost play.

108a *the rites and observances followed here*: probably sacrifices made where three roads meet. Such practices belonged to the cult of Hecate, a goddess of the underworld, who was associated with magic and was worshipped at crossroads.

108d *the skill of Glaucus*: a proverbial expression, of uncertain origin, for the skill demanded by a difficult task.

109b *the Phasis River and the Pillars of Heracles*: the Phasis, which flowed into the eastern shore of the Black Sea, and the Pillars of Heracles (Gibraltar) lay at the eastern and western boundaries of the world inhabited by the Greeks.

109c *"ether"*: i.e. the sky, thought of as consisting of blue fire. The element is described in the *Timaeus* (58d) as a rarefied form of air. The physical elements of our world are mere residues or 'dregs' from the pure and beautiful constituents of the 'true earth' that Socrates is about to describe. By representing the world familiar to us as a poor by-product of the 'real' world, his geological theory serves to illustrate a major theme of the *Phaedo*; but it also shows Plato's eye for the wondrous beauty of the physical world itself.

110b *those twelve-piece leather balls*: play-balls made from twelve pieces of pliable leather, each in the shape of a regular pentagon, and sewn together to form a dodecahedron. This, when stuffed, would acquire the shape of a sphere.

112a *A great way off ... beneath earth*: *Iliad*, viii. 14.

115c *he imagines I'm that dead body*: Socrates here draws a striking distinction between his body and his 'true self'. See Introduction, p. xvi.

115e *misuse of words*: Plato often suggests that ordinary ways of speaking can mislead us. Compare 68c, 76a, 82b, 99b, 107c.

117a *ready-pounded in a cup*: the hemlock was prepared by pounding. A joking allusion to the process occurs in Aristophanes' *Frogs* 123. See also Pliny, *Historia Naturalis*, xxv. 95.

118a *we owe a cock to Asclepius*: Asclepius was the god of healing. Socrates' last words are usually taken to mean that death is, paradoxically, the cure for the illness of human life. But the idea of life as an illness, though once attributed to Cebes (95d), is hardly Socratic in spirit (see 90e–91a). It is possible that the words refer to a real obligation of unknown origin. For Socrates to charge Crito with the settlement of an actual debt would be in keeping with the closing words of the dialogue.

INDEX

The figures in bold type refer to the text of the *Phaedo*

INDEX